The Prison Ch
And Its Expe

Hosea Quinby

Alpha Editions

This edition published in 2024

ISBN 9789362517210

Design and Setting By
Alpha Editions
www.alphaedis.com
Email - info@alphaedis.com

Contents

PART I.   - 1 -

UNDER THE REFORMATORY SYSTEM.   - 2 -

PART II.   - 37 -

Under the Punitive and Money-making System.   - 38 -

CONCLUSION.   - 123 -

PART I.

UNDER THE REFORMATORY SYSTEM.

1. *Emotions at the idea of assuming the position, and object of these pages.* The proposal of friends that I become chaplain of our State Prison at first struck me with much disfavor, from the idea that the position, instead of affording the encouragement and satisfaction attendant upon my former labors in schools and churches, must be up-hill work, and repulsive to the finer feelings of the heart. Still, having been no little accustomed to laying aside personal tastes and conveniences for the good of others, I yielded, and commenced the work on the first Sabbath in July, 1869.

The experience gained in this connection, with the hints and suggestions on collateral subjects, is set forth in the following pages, not for the purpose of personal notoriety, but for the sake of correcting important misconceptions by giving the true facts, and making a humble effort towards awaking in the public mind a deeper interest on a subject in which every citizen should feel a concern, and on which he should become duly informed, and thus be prepared to act intelligently. For this preparation he needs light, which light the real working of things, properly set forth, would surely give. Experience is ever regarded as the best school-master, the proper touchstone to all our theories.

Never was the community more widely and deeply stirred than now on the questions, "What course will prove the most corrective of crime with the least public burden? What is the true method of managing penal institutions?"

These are questions of no trifling moment, questions which bear largely on the public weal. From the days of Howard, the philanthropist, they have been rising in the public estimate, now to stand among the more prominent of the age.

On these, widely differing theories are brought face to face in earnest antagonism; some contending for the sterner type of the vindictive, for rendering the condition of the wrong doer as repulsive as possible, thus to terrify him from erring,—others contending that they have found a better and more effective way in humane, reform, gospel efforts,—efforts prompted by the principles of enlightened Christianity.

The writer, while touching upon a somewhat wide range of points, will constantly aim at as great brevity in statement as may be consistent with perspicuity, go into detail only so far as shall appear needful to the end in view, and feel amply compensated for his labors, if the developments and suggestions here made shall in any degree aid the cause of prison reform.

2. *Our first meeting for worship.* In assembling, while the ladies and gentlemen, admitted from the city, were taking their places at my left and front, the female prisoners were being arranged at my right, closely facing the wall, with the matron and assistant beside them, that they might not indulge in looking about upon others, for such an act was held as a misdemeanor. This done, and the south door securely bolted, that leading to the hall was unbarred, and the male prisoners, some one hundred and twenty, were marched in by divisions and regular file, taking their seats with perfect order before me, and filling every available foot of otherwise unoccupied space in that small and ill ventilated room called "the chapel," thus packing it as closely apparently as could be.

What a sensation thrilled every nerve on this my first experience in attempting to dispense the gospel, thus locked within walls of granite and iron, with a military guard at each window ready to deal summarily with any who should attempt escape, or commit a disorderly act. Then what mingled emotions of sorrow and pity at the thought of so great an amount of talent present, which had been devoted to crime, and the depths to which their iniquities had sunk the wrong doers,—enough to make angels weep.

The singing by the prison choir, a young lady of the city presiding at the instrument, was exhilarating, voices good, all in time, and movement spirited, the whole having a peculiar charm. Many a choir outside might have listened with advantage. The Scripture reading was responsive, the chaplain repeating a verse and then the audience. As the speaker commenced his sermon, every convict's eye was fastened upon him, apparently with the deepest interest, continuing thus to the close.

This fixed attention, with all the connected circumstances, acted as a powerful stimulus to his intellect and heart, causing thoughts and words to flow almost unbidden, and those of a peculiar unction, thus rendering preaching in the place easy. The numerous moistened eyes and earnest countenances seemed plainly to say, "Here are minds responsive to the truth, a field which can be cultivated for God and humanity."

Those anticipated feelings of repulsion did not arise, but rather the assurance that success and pleasure would attend a faithful dispensing of the word for reforming and elevating the prisoner in his bonds, as well as in efforts to save sinners under more favorable surroundings.

3. *The Sabbath School.* This met Sabbath afternoon in two places, the females, eight in number, in their work room, with the matron and other ladies who might attend from the city as teachers; the males in the chapel, a number of

Christian ladies and gentlemen from outside attending and hearing classes, some having long been laborers here in the work, one having, years previous, helped set the school in operation. The toils of these earnest workers were evidently being blessed, under God, to the good of their pupils, producing impressions upon some, which greatly aided them in their efforts at reform. My attendance was with the latter, and the interest was fully equal to that I had witnessed in the forenoon worship.

The prisoners were required to attend the latter, while the Sabbath school attendance was left to the inmates as a voluntary matter, and yet some ninety males attended this, about three-fourths of the whole company from which the audience was usually drawn,—a much larger percentage probably than any outside congregation can boast of.

4. *General appearance of the convicts.* Judging from appearance as they sat in the assembly, a few were evidently hard cases, narrow-minded, sordid, ugly. To a number, dame Nature had dealt bountifully on the score of mind, they having noble foreheads, and bright, sparkling eyes, indicative of no small natural ability. One would think that some of these would have shone conspicuously in any of the learned professions, business circles, or common industries of life had they bent their minds in the right direction. Certain visitors at the prison and State House, in time of the legislative session, were wicked enough to say that they found the likelier appearing company at the former place. Other inmates partook more of the low cunning, the artful, leading them to accomplish their ends by more adroit means, while a small number seemed bordering on insanity, two on idiocy.

In dealing with these, as a whole, while at large, no doubt the police had found their own shrewdness, at times, keenly taxed, and been made to feel that they were called to grapple with mind worthy of a better cause.

5. *The warden.* He was found to be a man of generous impulses, an earnest Christian worker, with a heart full of kindness, professing to act for the prisoners' highest good. He would furnish them with enough of suitable food, good clothing and bedding, all needed care in sickness, with the requisite means for mental, moral and religious improvement, fully believing in the practicability of labor to reform the wayward and elevate the fallen, that reform is the primary purpose of the institution. As one great means to this, he seemed to feel it needful that the inmates be kept under strict, wholesome discipline, and required at all times, when able, to perform their tasks fully and faithfully.

He was accustomed to hold correspondence with other prison officers of like faith with himself on prison management, and profited by any feasible hints thus gained. His motto was, "Keep the prisoners on good fare, provide them all needed means for reform and make all the money practicable from the prison as subordinate to these."

6. *Educational means found in operation.* By the combined effort of the warden and my predecessor, what we may term a secular school had been established in the chapel, to be held evenings, in sessions of one hour each, as often as a guard could be spared from other prison duties. This was voluntary on the part of these gentlemen, and was intended to be open for all the male prisoners of good behavior to attend, and take such of the common branches as each should need.

The legislature had so far recognized the move as to vote the chaplain an increase of salary in consideration of his labors as teacher in the school. But here it stopped, and that short of its full duty. It ought to have gone further, and made the thing a fixed fact, obligatory upon all prison officers, as really as our common school system outside is upon town officers. Why not? The State has taken the convicts under her care as wards, moved them from their vicious surroundings, and put them where, with a little additional painstaking on her part, many of these may be led to the daily habit of devoting their otherwise idle or squandered moments to storing up valuable ideas for future use, a long step towards their true reform.

As leading in the same direction, these gentlemen had adopted the custom of having occasional lectures in the chapel for the men by outside speakers, also readings by a lady elocutionist, and meetings for instruction and drill in singing.

7. *Influence left by the former chaplain.* This influence was of a highly salutary character among the prisoners. A number would feelingly refer to his efforts for their best being, and from which they had been constantly striving to profit. Some professed to have experienced a change of heart under his ministration, and were still living in the exercise of daily Bible reading and prayer, being obedient prisoners, duly attentive to all the prison rules, and in good repute among the officers of the institution. They continued thus till leaving prison, and had not fallen from their integrity when last heard from. Eternity alone can unfold the amount of good secured to those once degraded men by these efforts.

8. *Prison order.* While intent on reform measures, we were not for a moment to lose sight of the strictest order. The warden would have the rounds for this carefully observed, that no risk should be run with regard to the safe keeping of the prisoners and their due observance of the rules. Hence, the chaplain was not allowed to hold his school in the chapel for instructing the men, or have any gathering of prisoners there without a guard. Then, previous to their admittance, we were required to be certain that the south door to the chapel was securely fastened, and the key, for safe keeping, passed through an opening to the guard-room. And when the exercises were ended, and the men secured in their cells, on a given signal, the keeper of the key would open for our release.

This order was not to be deviated from under any circumstances. From this fact, had the prisoners, at any time, risen in rebellion, overpowered the guard and chaplain, they would have found no means in the room for escaping. Or had any professed goodness, or pretended to a great desire for education with the hope of being taken to the chapel under circumstances favorable to their getting away, they would have found it of no avail. Good or bad, professedly reformed or not, all were treated alike in this respect. And, so far as I had the opportunity of observation, the same strictness was observed in all other departments of the prison.

True, one escaped, but from no lack of internal watchfulness or order. His time had almost expired, he having been a faithful, obedient, well-disposed prisoner. The warden set him at work doing chores about the stable and outer yard, not supposing that he would leave for so short a period, and thereby forfeit his commutation and render himself liable to be returned at any time through life. But after serving here a few days he absconded.

---

9. *Chaplain's routine of duty.* In this were embraced, not only the Sabbath morning service and the Sabbath school care, but also visiting the cells for giving words of advice, visiting the hospital for imparting religious consolation, managing the secular school, changing the library books for the inmates, Saturdays, learning, from the prisoners, enough of their past history to enable him to judge of the instruction adapted to each, and, in fine, to speak such words here and there as would conduce to the requisite order. This gave a wide range, an important field. I seemed to have returned to my school keeping days; and found my long habit of reading human nature in students of no little use, aiding me to understand the best manner of approaching each so as to gain his confidence. Also my custom in school discipline, which had at times been complained of as being too strict, now served an excellent purpose, prompting me, at every step, to move in decided contrariety to all irregularity and disorder.

10. *General description of the prison and prison management.* The old part of the prison was erected in 1812, favored by Mason, Woodbury and other distinguished men of that day, the avowed purpose being to have an institution where the criminals of the State could be gathered and put under reformatory influences. Thus it appears that the idea of reform was a fundamental one in the founding of the establishment. Some years since the north wing, for the male prisoners, was erected, which is three-storied and contains 120 cells, each about three and one-half feet wide, seven feet long and seven high, the bedsteads being of iron and made to turn up. The south wing, or old part, contains a tenement for the deputy and cells for the female prisoners.

The warden occupies the main building, or middle part. Here, too, are the cook room for the male prisoners, the chapel, the office, guard room, hospital, dormitories for the guards and overseers, and the reception room, in which the library is kept.

The prison yard is surrounded on three sides by a granite wall, perhaps sixteen feet high, the prison itself constituting the wall on the fourth side. In the yard are two buildings of brick, each two stories high, one much larger than the other: the smaller, on its lower floor, affording a wash-room, tailor's shop, &c., the second story and attic rooms used for storage or any needed mechanical purpose, sometimes as shoe shops; the larger building is devoted to bedstead manufacturing, the machinery driven by steam.

From this engine these two buildings are warmed by means of steam pipes, the boiling in the wash-room being done by the same. The hall is furnished with a steam boiler, which not only warms that, but also the guard and reception rooms, and the chapel, and the steam is used in the men's cook room, all other warming and heating in the prison being done by wood fires. To economize fuel as much as possible, a steam pipe has been extended from the engine room to the prison to conduct the waste steam of the shop boilers for use in those apartments.

The female prisoners eat at a table in the warden's kitchen and from the same food as goes to his own table. The men have a prescribed diet, called rations, the allowance of each being dealt out in a tin basin,—meat, potatoes, gravy, &c., all together, the potatoes unpared. Coffee is given in a tin dipper. The meals being ready, the men are marched through an entry by a long table standing contiguous to the kitchen and loaded with their rations, each taking what belongs to him, carrying it to his cell and partaking in solitude. Their mode of eating is quite a curiosity. They generally use their beds for tables, and each has a knife, fork and spoon in his cell of which he takes the exclusive care. He fishes out his potatoes and pares them; but where shall he put the parings, dripping as they are? He has no extra dish. Then how shall he wash his knife, fork and spoon? He can use his tongue, for he has nothing else, and he may or may not have a towel on which to wipe them, but his jacket sleeve or pants' leg is wonderfully convenient.

What a dehumanizing system! Why not let the men eat at tables the same as the women, and have some decency about the matter? Then how much better in another respect. By the present system, rations must be dealt out to all alike, giving the same quantity to each, with the result of having more or less food returned or a part not have enough, some eating more than others. But if at a table, each can eat as he needs, and thus avoid suffering or waste.

The men are provided with means for ablution by a few bathing-troughs in their wash-room. An old man gave me quite an amusing description of the operation, thus: "The bathing department here is a wonderful institution. They will march a file of men into the wash-room, old and young together, fill the troughs with water, put in a little soap, then a nigger or two to grease it with; when done, the men must strip and go in one after another. A wonderful institution! I never would go that."

The female prisoners are employed in mending and making apparel for the men, and in domestic labors in the family apartment. The feeble men are employed in light work about the hall, such as dusting, carrying water to the cells, whitewashing, sweeping, &c., or in repairing clothes. Two able-bodied men are required in the cook room, another in the wash-room and to do chores, and part of the time still another. The remaining men are let to a contractor, who pays a stipulated price per day for each when he works.

The needed officers to the institution are the warden, deputy, physician, chaplain, hospital steward, four overseers, four guards, and two night watchmen, fifteen at least. All of these must be paid from the prison earnings. When to this is added the cost for supporting the prisoners, the ordinary repairs, printing the Report and annual apprisal, we have the net prison gain. But the outsets, with the strictest economy, must always of necessity be large, showing that crime is an important drawback to industry and thrift.

When I commenced my labors at the institution, it was about emerging from an experience which had brought no little opposition to the warden from some in the city, especially in the line of his reform moves.

He took the prison in '65, the inmates, numbering seventy, being let on a contract of forty cents per day; the bedding extremely limited; the cells swarming with those pestiferous attendants on sleeping hours, every crevice between the stones and bricks affording a safe resort; the food for the inmates insufficient for prison demands.

He at once commenced a war of extermination in the cells. Having secured a change of bedding, and taking a division at a time, he would remove all the articles for washing and boiling, and inject burning fluid into the cracks and crevices, setting fire to it, and thus literally burning out each apartment. He found it essential to renew this attack, however, as months rolled round.

Finding, from the best authority at hand on prison fare, that it is not safe to run the supply to a man lower than twenty cents per day in cost for the raw material as the market usually is, and that flour bread is an economical food for prisoners, as well as being humane, he resolved to adopt this with a diet commensurate with nature's real demands, built a baker's oven, and hired a baker for instructing certain selected inmates in the art of baking, and established the daily supply seen in the Bill of Fare at the end of this article. Under the head of "vegetables" are embraced all the articles commonly used as such on our tables,—onions, beets, carrots, parsnips, turnips and cabbage. Not, however, using all at any one meal.

In the chapel service the warden gave the prisoners liberty to look upon the speaker,—a great relief from the former downcast method,—and the chaplain introduced the responsive manner of reading, denounced by some as a most dangerous innovation. The Sabbath school was held the year round, instead of simply during the session of the legislature, and a few months beside.

But it required close calculation and strict economy with the warden to meet the current expenses with the wages of forty cents per day to a man, though he did that and gained a little.

The war ending, the tide began to set towards the institution, increasing the number in '66 to 111, '67 to 118, and '68 to 135, the highest number ever reached by the institution. The current then turned, the prisoners numbering in '69, 129, and in '70, 118.

In '67 the authorities relet the prisoners at ninety cents per day instead of forty, a great advance, brightening the financial prosperity of the institution. But in doing this they had to make a great outlay in enlarging the shop, obtaining a new engine, boilers, &c. There were, also, important repairs, with improvements in the drainage and ventilation, made.

These outlays were mostly made by the warden, the Governor, for the time, assenting and advising. In '69 the Governor and council relieved the warden of all financial responsibility, appointing one of their number to act as prison agent, and make the purchases and meet the outlays at the prison, in which year they put a new roof to the south wing and made other important alterations and repairs. From the legislative grants and prison earnings all these expenses were met, and the year closed with the institution free of debt, in good repair, and with all needed labor appliances, which was a great relief to all having the care and responsibility of the concern, rendering the task of keeping things tidy and in comfortable order much easier than formerly. It is better and more economical for the State. That constant patching up and fixing over in numerous places, swallowing up money, no one hardly knowing how, is now nearly ended, permitting the real gains of the institution to accumulate and stand prominently in view, though everything there is not quite perfection yet.

The drainage and ventilation were found very defective and in bad order, but by the remodeling are made as good, perhaps, as can be in the situation.

In this general fitting up, the prison officers and men voluntarily contributed to quite an extent, of which no account anywhere appears, though the State enjoys the gain. In the summer and fall of '69 and the spring of '70, I frequently saw the deputy, out of the usual work hours, going with squads of men to labor on the sewers or wherever they could advantageously.

The prison is lighted by gas. In the hall the burners, thirty-two in number, are placed along the outer walls, each from eight to ten or twelve feet from a cell, but being old and leaking badly, they give a poor light, the bars to the cells casting shadows on the books or papers the prisoners may attempt to read. Hence, one of the governors ordered candles to be furnished to the cells extra when desired. These were so extensively called for that in '69 the gas had been largely dispensed with for the candles.

In case a prisoner is attempting to run away, or is rising upon an officer, the officers are held at liberty to shoot, knock down, or use whatever means may be needed in self-defense or in preventing their escape. Otherwise prison rule does not allow an officer to strike a man, but he must be punished by the solitary or ball and chain at the discretion of the warden, who found it needful to use no little precaution as to the length of the former, "for too great severity in that tended to insanity on the part of the punished."

In letting the prisoners on contract, the State furnishes the shop to the contractor rent free, also the motive power, shafting and belting, keeping these in repair.

In managing the prisoners, each officer has his assigned position and duty, and everything is conducted with a precision closely approximating that of a military character.

The south door to the chapel, spoken of, opens to the female part in the south wing and to the pass-way down two nights of stairs and out of doors.

BILL OF FARE

At New Hampshire State Prison.

SUNDAY:
Breakfast—Baked beans, brown bread, and coffee.
Supper—Rice pudding, brown bread, and coffee.
MONDAY:
Breakfast—Flour bread, brown bread, and coffee.
Dinner—Corned beef, vegetables, and brown bread.
Supper—Flour bread, molasses, and coffee.
TUESDAY:
Breakfast—Corned beef, warm brown bread, and coffee.
Dinner—Codfish, potatoes, butter gravy, and brown bread.
Supper—Flour bread, molasses, and coffee.
WEDNESDAY:
Breakfast—Fish hash, brown bread, and coffee.
Dinner—Fresh beef soup with vegetables, and brown bread.
Supper—Flour bread, molasses, and coffee.
THURSDAY:
Breakfast—Meat hash, brown bread, and coffee.
Dinner—Stewed peas with pork, and brown bread.
Supper—Flour bread, molasses, and coffee.
FRIDAY:
Breakfast—Meat hash, warm brown bread, and coffee.
Dinner—Baked fresh fish or chowder, potatoes, and brown bread.
Supper—Flour broad, molasses, and coffee.
SATURDAY:
Breakfast—Meat hash, brown bread, and coffee.
Dinner—Fresh beef soup with vegetables, and brown bread.
Supper—Flour bread, molasses, and coffee.

———

11. *General remarks upon the prisoners.* When entering my service here, the prison had more inmates than cells. Eight were females. The community was reaping a sad harvest from the demoralizing effects of the late war. Six or eight were U. S. prisoners.

All treated me with due respect. The most were easily approached, free in conversation, readily giving account of themselves, admitting their crimes and the justice of their sentences, which probably they would not have done to one in whom they could not confide. A very few would plead innocence, some, no doubt, rightfully; three probably having been victims of fiendish plots. Two or three were very reticent, one saying, "No one here shall ever know my real name, native place, or business of life."

It was heart-sickening to listen to their tales of wrong and suffering, clearly showing that "the way of the transgressor is hard." Sin has a most debasing effect upon its victims. Three-fourths or more doubtless came to prison directly or indirectly through strong drink. True, in many cases, more remote causes lay back of this, a native inclination to sin, loss of parents, parental neglect, family infidelity, vicious associates, ignorance, Sabbath-breaking and the like. A very few had used no strong drink. A large share were young, some mere boys on their alternate sentence. Many, on entering, could neither read nor write.

The crimes were various, extending from the worst murder cases down to the lower grades of iniquity, some perfectly fiendish, horrible. It would seem impossible for men and women to do such deeds.

But these inmates were evidently not all the wrong doers of the State who merited punishment. In a few cases, no doubt, the prosecutor rather deserved the doom. Then there are those rum-sellers, keepers of billiard saloons, gambling dens, and houses of ill fame, all inciting to crime. Numbers of them stand really in the light of *particeps criminis* to our inmates, and perhaps were more deserving of this confinement. How long will the people see this class making criminals of our sons and brothers, yea, of our daughters and sisters too, and remain inactive? Why do not the very stones cry out?

I found all the prominent religious persuasions here represented, from the Universalist to the staid Quaker; a number had been Sabbath school attendants, one quite an Advent speaker, who seemed positive he would be able to convert us all to his notions could he have the stand for a suitable time, a privilege he earnestly strove for. More came from the Catholics than from any other sect, and more from the shoe-makers than from any other business class.

When introducing the subject of personal piety to each, no little care was required to bring it forward in such a manner that it should not strike the mind repulsively, and thus fill it with needless prejudice, but rather conciliate and convince, leading to free conversation upon the subject. In this a great advantage would be gained.

The larger portion acceded to the just claims of religious truth upon them, some hoping that their imprisonment was being sanctified to their highest good. One feelingly said, "I was swiftly floating on the stream of sin and corruption towards that awful gulf in which I must have landed ere this, had not the prison walls caught and saved me, as I trust." Some I found professing a belief in infidelity, a few in real atheism.

As weeks passed on, it became evident that something beyond human power was at work in the minds of a few. Personal conversation developed the fact that they were really and seriously considering their ways. A case of much hope would occasionally present itself. "But," says one, "these fellows were professing this with the hope of getting out."

That could not have been the case with some, most surely, as their term had nearly expired and they neither asked nor looked for a pardon. The work must have been genuine with these, if not with all. Nor could I see any reason to doubt the sincerity of any, and I scrutinized closely.

The classification of prisoners, as to their crimes, affords an interesting subject. It will be largely found that the wrong doing of each is of a specific character rather than a general. Thus that of one is simply in the line of murder; that of another, robbery; of a third, stealing, or picking pockets, acting the burglar, assaulting female character, or of whatever sort. Then, thieves can be classified into horse thieves, sheep stealers, leather thieves, watch and money thieves, and so on.

Some commit crimes only when influenced by strong drink, and then steal, quarrel or murder. Many can not help their wrong doing, or will not, and therefore should remain in prison, where they can live as very good men, and aid the State instead of cursing society by their wrong deeds.

They do not all steal for the gain, but for the sake of stealing. Hence here is one who will hoard up his booty and never go to it afterwards. I asked an old man, a burglar, what induced him to lead such a life, and received this answer: "There is something peculiarly exciting in the engagements. I never engaged in it for what I could obtain."

---

12. *Prayer meetings commenced.* Previous to the present fall, no prayer meetings had been established at the prison, the need of which we now greatly felt. After much thought on the matter, I asked the warden if we could not introduce them, and he answered, "Oh no, that can't be. There are so many hypocrites among the prisoners, who would take advantage to say what they might choose, and to the disgust of the others, that we can not control the matter." This came from no lack of interest in the subject, for it was the very thing that had found a large place in his contemplations and desires, though he had seen no time when he could feel it safe to take the step. Not being able to put the idea out of mind, I soon brought it before him again, but in connection with the Sabbath school teachers. After duly considering the pros and cons, the question was decided thus,—"Start such a meeting,

to be held weekly, if found practicable. Next Sabbath let each teacher, when hearing his class, select such of the number as he may think fitted for the exercise; passing the names to the warden for him to invite them in at his discretion, the meeting to commence the following Monday evening."

To prepare their minds for the occasion, the discourse, the next Sabbath, was on hypocrisy, the text being the account of Ananias and Sapphira, with the attempt to point out the enormity and danger of that sin, that the truly sincere should not be kept from duty by hypocrisy as seen in others, or by being accused of it in themselves by the malicious. At the close, the warden, grasping my hand, said, "We will let all go in who choose. We will make no selection," and we appointed the meeting accordingly.

Met at the time appointed, nearly one hundred being present, for it was a novel matter there. In the commencement I clearly stated what would be expected of all who might engage in prayer or speaking, referring to the subject of the sermon the past day, and said that the opportunity was offered for those only to improve who sincerely desired to become better and were truly determined to act accordingly, expressing the full conviction that none would presume to come forward under any hypocritical pretenses.

A few of the Sabbath school teachers present took part to good acceptance. Then two or three of the inmates offered prayer, and three or four spoke of their feelings and desires. They could not have been more appropriate in their words, spirit, or manner. To all appearances they were sincere.

Perfect order prevailed,—a most profound and respectful attention. Much of the time the dropping of a pin upon the floor could have been heard. An overpowering spirit seemed to pervade the room, not so much in the words uttered as in the convictions of each man's own heart, it was an impressive season. How was my soul relieved at this triumph over our fears and rejoiced at the way God had evidently opened before us.

Thus the meetings commenced and that too indicating, as the first results, the very blessing I had been hoping and praying for, a deeper impressiveness to our Sabbath and other religious efforts. Shortly after, we found that hearts not sensibly touched before, were being deeply impressed, among them one of the worst cases perhaps in prison. It was taking a new start in the right direction.

In laboring with these men now, as at all times, I felt that a great responsibility rested on me; that this was no place for dealing softly, petting them with insinuations that they had been more sinned against than sinning, and that nothing was needed for them but a professed determination to amend, with a few efforts in that direction. Duty seemed imperative that I should labor to bring the wrong doings of each as clearly and impressively as could be before him, how deeply he had sinned against his own best good, his fellows and his God, enforcing the absolute necessity of true repentance, and turning to the right through faith in Christ; that he must make a thorough, radical work of the matter, or it would avail nothing. Thus plainly, yet coupled with a feeling heart, I invariably met the prisoners on these subjects. And where no evidence could be found of a realizing sense of sins committed and true compunction therefor, we could found no hope in the case.

13. *Pike, the Hampton murderer.* On entering, I found him in prison, not at work, but confined to his cell according to our present law, that, when one is condemned to execution, he shall be confined in the State Prison one year, at the end of which the sentence shall be carried out, unless receiving a reprieve or commutation.

By law also, the criminal has the right to choose his own spiritual adviser, and, much to my relief, I found that Pike had arranged with my predecessor about this before he left. Still I volunteered to the doomed man all the aid in my power, for which he appeared highly grateful.

The plea of insanity had been used on the trial, or that the accused was in a state of mind, when committing the offense, that rendered him irresponsible for the crime alleged, which plea Pike would ever make to me, sometimes alluding to the great injustice of his being hung. But as Mr. Holman had undertaken to fathom that, I never pressed him with any particular inquiry on the matter.

It would seem impossible for one manifesting the spirit Pike always did to us, to commit so horrid a crime, and probably he never would had he been free from rum. In prison, he at all times appeared gentlemanly and kind-hearted, helped me a number of days in repairing the library, and seemed glad of the opportunity.

When laboring with those he afterwards murdered, he was uniformly pleasant, ready to do anything for them they needed. They parted on the most friendly terms, the old people earnestly urging him to continue with them still longer.

But when Pike was under the influence of liquor, he was a very different man, and at times a highly dangerous character. In this he was fully responsible, for he could have let the drink alone, and did when he chose. I saw nothing leading me to doubt his full responsibility in the murder. But others also are responsible,—those who helped him to his liquor and thus caused his madness. Against them, also, the blood of those mangled forms cries loudly from the ground to a righteous God for vengeance. The community likewise, which, by supineness and inactivity, permitted those persons to carry on their nefarious traffic, must come in for its share. The blame of that startling act does not all lie at Pike's door, though he was guilty enough.

When I attempted to urge upon him the importance of a full preparation for the dread event before him, he seemed strangely inclined to put it off and almost callous to the magnitude of his sin. He would admit that his career had been one of desperate wickedness, but did not appear truly moved in spirit by its real enormity, or as having genuine repentance over the matter, a thorough breaking up of the fallow ground of the heart. Trusting to the idea of his non-responsibility as a shielding circumstance, he no doubt felt almost perfect confidence, till near the last, that a pardon, or commutation, would be granted, and ventured on that assurance. I constantly discouraged the idea, repeatedly urging him to put no confidence in that, but earnestly to set about a preparation for the worst. The final decision of the executive power, not to interfere with the decision of the court, came to me, but in such a way that I was not at liberty to announce it till officially divulged. Still, feeling so anxious for the criminal, I went as far as the circumstances would allow, and said to him, "From what I hear, your case is finally decided, but not in your favor. And I am perfectly satisfied that my information is reliable." But it was not official, and the very fact of its being withheld inspired him with hope that I was mistaken.

The rulers, no doubt, did as they thought best in the matter, but it would seem that there was an error on their part in not communicating their finality to the criminal as soon as made. It was a grave matter to him, and the last few days he reflected no little upon the course.

In our labors with the doomed man, we had two prominent points before us, one to fit his mind for going upon the gallows with the needed fortitude, the other to lead him to a due preparation for appearing before his God. During the last week, by his desire, clergymen from the city visited him. A few of the singers from the city, also, by the warden's invitation, occasionally called and spent a short time with him, singing some of those devotional pieces so well fitted to his case, which were followed by prayer and then all retired. His cell was now in the hall. This occurred when the other prisoners were in the shop at work, for at no other time were visitors allowed at his cell. Two or three of his last days were spent in the hospital, which then had no sick occupant. The strictest care and watchfulness were observed by the officers, so that, whether in his cell or in the hospital, he could not possibly escape if he attempted it.

The day appointed for the execution was Tuesday. Monday the criminal frankly admitted to his adviser, that he knew what he was doing that terrible night, and was fully responsible for the deed, which acknowledgment he signed in writing. He also dictated a letter to his youngest brother, faithfully warning him against following his own ways of wildness and drinking, also a note containing good advice to two young men who had been officers in the prison, and finally an address to be read on the scaffold. Brothers and other relatives took leave of him Monday afternoon and Tuesday morning.

The fatal hour was fixed at eleven, A. M. Pike was up in due season, took a slight morning repast, dressed for the day, had devotional exercises, and finished parting with friends at nine, that he might have opportunity for becoming duly rested and composed in mind for that painful occasion. At ten the other officers retired, leaving him alone with us two. What an hour before us? I had never experienced the like before and hope never to again. It was much like standing on the crumbling verge of time and looking into eternity's vast abyss.

We had a season of prayer, then conversation for the purpose of learning his present feelings and convictions. He professed a hope that God had forgiven his sins and would accept him at last; said that no doubt it would be better for him to go then than be pardoned and return to the world once more, for, in that case, his appetite might overpower him again and he do other horrid deeds. Still, it was hard to die in the way he must.

Personal conversation over, we continued bringing to his mind fitting portions of Scripture and appropriate verses from hymns and thus occupied the moments till eleven slowly arrived.

Our door opens. The sheriff with his attendants enters. We march to the scaffold in the hall, where are gathered many reporters for the press and other gentlemen. The address being read and prayer offered, Mr. Holman at his right and myself at his left lead him upon the fatal drop, and there support him while the preparation for the last is being made. During the adjustment of the black cap and noose, I feel a tremor in his arm. He is taken forward from us and placed under the beam. His legs are bound, his arms pinioned, the sheriff reads extracts from the doings of the court, and gives the final sentence. The spring is touched, the drop falls, the surgeon calls for the rope to be drawn higher, as the feet touch the floor. This done, life ends in about a quarter of an hour.

As the drop fell, Mr. Holman settled back in a chair, faint. I led him to a window where he soon recovered, but serious illness followed, caused by the excitement and anxiety of his labors here.

Now, if men must be hung, humanity would call for the work to be performed differently in these respects: That mortal long reading from the court doings should be dispensed with, that is, long for the place. It can be of no sort of use. A short formula, consisting of the last two or three sentences, uttered by the sheriff, would be all sufficient.

Then, again, that black cap should be different. Binding the limbs consumed a few moments, and the reading, referred to, still more. But probably after the cap was on and the noose fitted over it, the criminal exhausted all the oxygen available to him in three or four breaths, and was forced to suffer the process of suffocation during that occupied time. How near death he was when the drop fell, I can not say, but he appeared to be suffering greatly before the binding was completed. That could all be remedied by having an orifice in the cap opposite the mouth for breathing.

Further, that sad mistake about the rope should never be allowed to happen. He who permits himself to be appointed to such a duty, ought so to understand his business that such an accident shall be impossible.

Some of the papers, especially in New York, roughly criticised our efforts to prepare Pike for his end, said it was an outrage on society to give a wretch like him so much attention; that, in it, we exhibited a sickly sentimentalism, appeared as though we would raise crime to a saintship, and more in the same line. A few words only on this must suffice.

We supposed that the sentiment, "The criminal has a right to the benefit of the clergy," really meant something; that, though this man had been condemned to execution by his compeers for a most outrageous crime, he yet had a right to means for preparing himself to pass the ordeal of the scaffold with due composure, and for becoming reconciled to his God, if that could be. We did not dream that anybody short of heathendom would object to this. Supposing we were appointed to work for that end, we went to the task with a sincerity of purpose. If we were not appointed to do just the things we did, for what were we, pray?

We simply followed the usual course pursued at the bedside when one is near death, had religious conversation, prayer, singing, parting with friends; though, in this case, we had no extreme feebleness caused by disease to meet, but rather crime, in one of its most revolting forms, to recognize in bringing gospel appliances, concerning which crime we endeavored to be duly faithful.

Hence, all that feverish editorial brain-work over this pretended wrong, and that amount of printer's ink and paper thus used were simply wasted upon, what never occurred, or that which was only a usual, honest effort to do our duty with fidelity.

But this tirade, no doubt, came through the agency of some living not far away, who designedly put a newsmonger on the wrong scent, for the purpose of venting their own spleen at the idea of having those around who would treat a helpless, fallen man better than a dog.

---

14. *Doctrinal discourses.* In pursuing my labors among the prisoners, I often met those skeptical views, before alluded to, which were sometimes quite boldly avowed. Some of them would constantly attend the Sabbath school, doubtless simply from the pleasure derived in puzzling their teachers with questions. They were acute, shrewd fellows, keen in argument, quick to see a point and turn it, hard to meet. To help these, if possible, I decided to give a few discourses on the evidences of the existence of a God as seen from the light of nature. Those of the skeptical class as well as others manifested no little interest in the subject. Soon evidences began to appear of a material softening among them in their opposition to Bible truths. One young man said to the warden, "When the chaplain commenced those discourses, I felt sure of being impregnably fixed in my ideas. After hearing one, I would retire to my cell and sit down with the purpose of figuring out the want of conclusiveness in his arguments. But the more I figured, the more I saw that I was in the wrong and not he; that, from what we see all about us, there must be a God, whom I am convinced I ought to love and obey." This man became altogether changed in his habits and entered upon a really hopeful course. Nor was he alone among those thus yielding, who had long been accustomed to shut their eyes against the true light.

---

15. *Effect of the prayer meeting on prison order.* These meetings had now continued a number of weeks with no abatement of interest, having gained the reputation of being the best in the city. But it became needful for us, at this time, to suspend all our chapel exercises for a while, to give place to the proposed enlargement of the room. Hence, at the close of the last meeting previous to this vacation, the warden said, in substance, "We have been holding these meetings several weeks. At first I thought them wholly impracticable in the place, but am truly glad to find I was so greatly mistaken. As an act of simple justice, I feel that I ought to bear testimony, before you all, to the influence they have exerted on the morals of the inmates. Since they commenced, we have not had a single case for discipline in this institution, a fact without precedent in the past, so far as my knowledge extends, for so long a time. And I most devoutly hope that this state of things will continue and the meetings grow more and more powerful in their influence for good."

Such a result of our efforts was in advance of what I had dared hope for. Though fully convinced that the influence must be in that direction, I had not realized so clearly that we were setting in operation what would prove so effective an aid to order in the prison.

---

16. *The new chapel.* At length the chapel was completed and made a gem of a room, as it seemed to us, in comparison with what it previously was, having been enlarged to nearly double its former size, extending the whole width of the building and taking in the windows on both sides, thus giving us great improvement in air and general comfort; the painting also was neat and cheerful. We all felt truly thankful for so great a blessing, thankful, too, for the opportunity of meeting again to resume our worship. As the poor fellows entered, one after the other, and cast their eyes about upon the beauty and neatness before them, I could see the joy flash over their countenances. The singing sent a new thrill to the heart, and it seemed much easier to speak to them. Everything appeared more hopeful for good.

During the recess, I had been assiduous in visiting the prisoners, Sabbaths and other days, and endeavoring to influence them in the right. But now that the meetings had commenced, we could rationally look for a greater success to our efforts.

Nor did we look in vain, for soon some professed a full determination to forsake their ways of sinning and seek to become what God required. These indications, as is usual in the outside world, tended to give the general moral tone, in the prison, a deeper impressiveness.

---

17. *Prison repairs and mistakes.* Previous to the enlarging of the chapel, general repairs and important alterations had been made in the south wing, consisting of a new French roof, a great improvement in appearance and utility, new cells for the female prisoners, and other rooms fitted for the officers and general prison use. The mechanics worked most diligently, and the money appropriated by the State was, no doubt, most economically laid out. The agent, one of the council, evidently felt no little satisfaction in having it said that he could accomplish so large amount of work with so little money.

But either he, or some one else, made at least two grave mistakes. One was in locating the cells for the females, which are in the third story, requiring the occupants, in going to and from their meals, and attending to much of their work, to pass over two, and sometimes three, flights of stairs. All understanding minds know that this must prey most sadly on female health, and that apartments for this class should be as near the ground as can be.

The other mistake was in the stairs. In the old arrangement the females had their private stairway, where they could pass unobserved by any except their attendants. But in the change, that private way was laid aside and the women required to use the public stairs, subjecting them to great inconvenience. I called the attention of the agent to this matter, but to no effect.

Another thing of trifling expense should have been attended to. The female wash-room should be arranged so that those laboring there, in turning out the waste water, should not be required to lift their tubs as high as, and, in some cases, higher than their heads; and, while washing, they should not be obliged to stand on ice so much. Blinds, also, should have been put to those large hospital windows to prevent almost broiling the sick in hot weather.

---

18. *Profanity attacked.* Profanity appeared to be a common evil in the institution, not only among the convicts, but also with many of those who were over them. A prisoner said to me one day, with no little emotion, "Chaplain, I am in a hard case. Swearing is my besetting sin. If I become vexed with my work, or anything else, that is my resort at once. In the meetings, I hear preaching, prayer and singing, under the influence of which, I feel a strong impulse to leave my sinful ways, and seek to become good and live an upright life. Almost resolved on this, I go to my work and am there forced to hear more or less profanity. They will swear at me, and I fall to swearing, too. Thus I am in a hard case." The deputy said, "There is swearing enough here daily to sink the whole concern clear down out of sight."

Thus assured, it seemed important that a move specifically against that sin be made. True, we might not reach those who most indulged in it, as they never attended our gatherings, but we could work for the prisoners. Hence, one evening, after speaking of the folly and sinfulness of the habit, an appeal was made direct to the men, soliciting all who would wholly abandon the practice to rise in their seats, to which some forty responded. At the next meeting, on requesting those who had succeeded in keeping their pledge to rise, the largest part signified their success. The next day as I passed about, some told me that, the past week, they had failed once or twice, but felt determined to struggle on and conquer. Subsequently one and another would assure me of their full triumph, that they had not been overtaken since that first week. How far the reform went, I shall never know, but it was in the right direction, such a reform as should be carried out everywhere, for no gentleman will take God's name in vain. It is a vulgar, mean practice.

19. *Efforts for a son, from a mother's plea.* During the spring of '71 and, while our religious interest was progressing, a mother visited her son in prison, having a temporary home with a lady friend in the city. We will call the mother, Mrs. A., the son, B., and the friend, Mrs. C.

Mrs. A., witnessing the subduing influences pervading our meetings, and feeling a strong desire that her son might be benefited thereby, determined to do what she could in that direction. This son was a youth who might have stood high, had he followed the right, but he had gone deeply into crime, causing his parents and friends untold sorrows. Still, this mother clung to him as only a mother can, hoping and praying for his rescue from his downward course.

The two families, here represented, had previously lived in near proximity and in happy union, when B. was an innocent youth, just emerging from childhood, a mother's pride and a father's hope. Considering this circumstance, and knowing that Mrs. C. had a class in the prison Sabbath school, and was an intelligent Christian worker, of good standing in the community, Mrs. A. conceived the idea that she perhaps might now essentially help her son, and solicited her to make the attempt. She replied, "I have no objection to attempting what I can to reclaim your son, with the warden's assent." This assent obtained, the two met in his presence. For a time B. appeared averse to talking directly of his convictions concerning the soul's interest. But she at length secured his confidence, thus leading him to speak of his feelings and desires to reform more freely, perhaps, than he had to the chaplain or warden. She referred to the past, what he once was, what his parents had done for him, what he might have been; to his fall, what he had lost, his present condition, his mother's agonized feelings in his behalf. The recital cut him keenly. Like Peter of old, he wept bitterly. She then pointed him to the Saviour as the only means of hope and relief. Thus she met him a few times and to good effect. He had been really interested in his religious welfare for a long time previous. But these efforts helped him greatly to decide fully to follow his convictions of duty. He became more alive to his true condition, perhaps, than ever before, would mourn over the heinousness of his sins, and evidently appeared to be drinking the bitter cup of repentance. He would be at times in real agony of mind at the view of himself.

While in this state, the warden invited those especially interested in the subject of religion to meet in the chapel, from twelve to twenty in number, for an inquiry meeting. We conversed with them severally and then proposed a season of prayer in which each should engage, which they did, B. among the rest, after which he appeared more calm, as if he had obtained a measure of relief, though he did not feel satisfied that he had really experienced a change of heart, but seemed decided about pursuing the right.

We encouraged him to press on as he had begun, and to take part in our meetings, to the latter of which he replied, "No, I will not attempt that. Should I, they will say, 'I am playing good with the hope of getting out.' That I won't do. I despise hypocrisy, however bad I may be in other things." Thus he took his stand, still interested in daily reading God's word, prayer, Sabbath school, and the general religious exercises. Other prisoners noted the change in him and would say, "He has been converted." But he was called to meet sore trials in the prison, trials hard to bear, of which we will speak hereafter.

---

20. *Warden's efforts for a young man.* This young man, here called E., from the middle walks of English society, parents well to do, with a good trade, superior mental powers, commanding high wages, came to this country to seek his fortune, fell into bad company, bad habits, and finally the State Prison. The warden became deeply interested in him, found that he was anxious about his religious state, and seeing the success of Mrs. C.'s labors invited Mrs. D. F., another prison Sabbath school teacher, resembling Mrs. C. in efficiency, character and standing, to make an effort with him for his good. She assented, and met him in the presence of the warden. She first took measures to satisfy herself that he was sincere and truthful with her, and proposed numerous questions about his home affairs, his history, &c. He answered her inquiries with apparent frankness, said that he was then under an alias, not wishing by his wrongs to disgrace his friends or real name, purported to give his true name, which she was not to reveal, the name of his minister and thus on. Mrs. D. F. had been acquainted with this minister, wrote to him, as she thought best, and in due time received an answer conclusively showing that E. had been truthful in his personal statements. She then conversed with him concerning his religious interests with about the same results as in the former case, except that he did not give so clear an evidence of a thorough work as did B.

The warden was particular to have the prison visits of these ladies in his presence, and sometimes that of the chaplain, too, not only that there should be no deviation from the rules of strict order, but also as a safeguard against evil reports. He well knew that there were ill-disposed persons who were ready to distort and misrepresent all his efforts at reform; and had a lady been admitted to private interviews with a prisoner, it would have given them just such stock to work with as would have delighted them.

---

21. *Experience with noble appearing heads in prison.*

Facts have shown that, in meeting an assembly, whether in prison or out, we can not always judge correctly in regard to the mental caliber of those composing it by the view of their heads. The apparent superior development may be deceptive, the work of disease. Among the "noble appearing heads" alluded to on a previous page, a part were of that class, or at least contained diseased minds. We will look at two cases, using substituted letters for the names, as previously.

H. is of good form, head finely proportioned, forehead high, eyes bright, all indicating, at a little distance, that he might possess no small share of intellect. Occasionally he will make pertinent, well timed remarks, but is greatly wanting in mental ability. I have been informed that his mother was intemperate, and had the delirium tremens just previous to his birth. He, also, years before, had at times appeared as though Satan himself possessed him, and was evidently insane, which, passing off, would leave him all right for a season. He has some remembrance of learning to read a little, can count almost one hundred, but has no power to combine numbers otherwise, at least none that I could find after persistent labor in drilling him almost daily for some four weeks on the same figures; thus, in addition table 8 and 1, 8 and 2, &c., ending where we commenced. Ask him, "How many are 8 and 2?" and he would as quickly answer, "11," or "9," as anything. Still he appeared earnest to learn, and was about twenty-four years old. He would detain me with him as long as possible to help him catch the idea, and would often say, "When I go out, I mean to find a good place where I can go to school, for I intend to obtain a good education." At times he would appear very religious, and talk and pray in our meetings; but, should anything irritate him, he perhaps would fly into a rage beyond all self-control, in which, if he could, he would kill a man as quickly as he would a fly. Still, an officer of the needed prudence and skill, by studying his infirmity and managing with due discretion, would have but little trouble with him, and he would readily earn his living. He would be an unsafe man to go at large, as dangerous, if fired with anger, as any raving maniac. He should ever be under firm control somewhere, with proper treatment and labor.

It would be difficult for us to determine how far moral responsibility can be affirmed of this man. God alone can decide that.

J. was another fine looking man of some twenty-eight years, gentlemanly appearing, with a good education, kindly disposed, usually of good habits, honest, so far as known, except in two cases, and those in much the same way. He would hire a team for a ride, go to a hotel and put up, exchange or sell the horse, or harness, or carriage, or all together, wander about awhile, and then return home for his father to help settle the matter, making no effort to escape arrest. The first time he was arrested, but not convicted, as neighbors pleaded in his behalf. The second time he was sent to prison. On this trial neighbors urged the father to put in the plea of insanity, but he refused, as so many were resorting to that. Still, all said that he had the best of reasons, as his own brother, or the young man's uncle died in an insane asylum, and those exceptional acts of his must have been performed through an insane impulse. Receiving a pardon previous to the close of his sentence, he went into good employment, worked steadily about a year, and took the same step again, when the court put him under guardianship, instead of sending him to prison, which was no doubt the most judicious course; for if kept from that horse hiring, he will doubtless be all right, as he has never manifested any inclination to wrong except in that particular point, and that only when his mind was evidently unhinged.

There were others who exhibited each his peculiarity. Some of these, could we look within their mental structure and there take a just survey, would perhaps be found possessed of such a native taint, or bias, or disorder, that their wrong doings, for which they were in prison, would be regarded in the light of misfortunes rather than crimes.

This subject of hereditary mental taint or disorder, in connection with wrong doing, opens to the phrenologist a wide and important field for investigation. But when he is forced to the conclusion that the one has acted from a disordered impulse of mind, uncontrollable, and he therefore not responsible for his acts, it can make no difference with the fact that the wrong doer must be restrained and put where he can not trespass upon the rights of others. It will rather lead to the questions of where he shall be confined, how employed, after what manner treated, and in what light regarded; perhaps showing clearly the need of important modifications in our present system of prison management.

---

22. *The Warden admits presents to prisoners from friends outside.* He would permit friends outside to send soothing dainties to the sick, or packages of fruit or home comforts to the well; or florists of the city to send bouquets to stand upon the speaker's desk on the Sabbath, for the prisoners to admire, and each received a flower or sprig to carry to his cell as a memento of innocence and purity, and a stimulus to love the Author of such beauty. It was really gratifying to see what cheer to the fallen these remembrances from the outside world would bring. All packages thus sent to prisoners were most carefully examined by officers, that nothing wrong should pass.

---

23. *Warden decides to resign.* He had not found his place a bed of roses. Certainly it possessed its thorns, and these, at times, largely predominated. His efforts for bringing the prison, in all its departments, to what it was, had cost him a great struggle, many anxious hours of planning, and at times perplexities in executing. But his greatest vexation came because of opposition, from certain ones without, to what he felt assured was for the best good of the institution, and from the misrepresentations of those opposed to all prison reform and improvement, who think it an outrage to the State to treat a prisoner better than a brute. He says one complained of him thus: "You give the prisoners too good fare, and make things too comfortable for them, on account of which they will wish to return. Whereas, the prison is a place for punishment, requiring you to keep the inmates on poorer food, and food so prepared that it shall be a punishment to eat it, and make everything around them a source of discomfort, that, after leaving, they may thereby be deterred from crime through dread of being returned."

From all considerations, the warden resolved to resign at the close of the year, yet, while remaining, to continue the usual prison rations and efforts at reform. His wife also heartily joined in his efforts, having from the first done much towards the excellent fare of the prisoners, and seeing that the sick were properly cared for. Hence, on one occasion, finding a man gradually wasting away with consumption, the skin wearing from his emaciated limbs by the hard prison couch, she sent in her own feather bed, that he might pass the remainder of his days in what comfort he could.

But what shall we think of the assertion that "the food should be so prepared that it shall be a punishment to the men to eat it?" Can it be possible, that one in New Hampshire, at this late day, uttered a sentiment like that? So the warden most positively asserts. To say nothing of its inhumanity, common worldly policy would repudiate such an idea. Of food thus prepared one at first would eat as little as possible to live, his powers for labor therefore depart, his appetite gradually fails, and he goes down to death.

All who use horses or oxen, except the worst of men, would scout such a practice. They say, "To have teams work well, feed well." So it must be with men, whether in prison or elsewhere. Power for muscular labor can be furnished only by generous food.

Then the fear that good prison fare would induce the prisoners to return purposely on recommitments, must have been expressed without due consideration, or being taught by prison facts. Statistics show that, where the prison is the most cruelly managed and the inmates are kept on the poorer fare, the greatest number return on second or third sentences.

Then as to our own prison, the very year this complaint was made, more pardons were granted, I think, than had ever been before in one year since the founding of the institution. And most surely none refused to accept of the offer and depart. Besides, nearly all who had friends, except those soon to go out by commutation, were constantly importuning them to intercede for their pardon, while those who had none, were persistent in their pleadings with the warden, chaplain and other prison officers to help them in efforts for the desired boon. Why this, if good fare would be an inducement to return? Would the utterer of that sentiment have sanctioned the idea of leaving the prison doors all unlocked and unbolted for one night? What a skedaddling there would have been, old or young, sick or well, the infirm and decrepit, hobbling off as best they could, leaving their good fare behind and their cells "to let."

What an idea! The good prison living, which at best can not be made equal to the comforts in our most common families outside, lead men to desire to be locked up in those gloomy cells for its sake and subjected to the general prison regime! That man may fear it who will.

24. *Prisoners' anxiety at the rumored resignation.* This rumor soon spread through the prison, not however to bring joy, but sorrow. I had not imagined that the prospect would cause the prisoners so much anxiety. Probably the slave of former days on the auction block, about to be struck off to a new owner, and all uncertain as to his future fate, would experience feelings allied to theirs. Their first anxiety seemed to be about their educational and religious privileges, lest these might be cut off or largely curtailed. Said one, "I have served on board of a whaleman and been accustomed to the most rigid discipline found there. I fear nothing in the line of strictness of rules, but can not bear the idea of being deprived of our school and meeting opportunities. I would do almost anything for the sake of enjoying these." This was the feeling.

Then, they were deeply anxious about the character of the man to be put over them, whether he would be humane, or the reverse. And no wonder, when we consider how completely they are left to his control. Probably no other state officer is so irresponsible as the warden of our state prison,— that is, in a position where those under him are so completely at his mercy, and where he can exercise real cruelty, if disposed, and cover it up with a fair outside show. None but a man of humane instincts, one especially qualified for the post, should be put in that position.

25. *Governor and Council memorialized by the prison S. S. teachers and chaplain.* Sustaining the relation we did to the prison, we thought it appropriate for us to set forth our views and desires to the Governor and Council touching the appointment of the warden; not respecting who should be appointed, but the principles to be secured. Hence, by a committee, we drew up a paper to be laid before them, giving account of the religious and educational privileges we had been laboring to secure to the inmates for the purpose of throwing around them all the influences possible for securing good order in the prison, and a preparation, on their part, for going out reformed, and duly prepared to act the part of good citizens, and also soliciting their honorable body, that they would so recognize these arrangements and labors of ours, in their contemplated appointment, that they should not be curtailed, but permitted to go on, gathering around them such improved facilities as might be devised from time to time, thus securing the best discipline in the prison and the highest ends of imprisoning.

We were treated on the occasions with due respect, and permitted to speak freely on the points as we judged best. Some of the gentlemen responded in most commendatory terms at what we had been doing, regarding the influence as highly salutary in regard to order and general good in the prison.

26. *Prison funerals.* The methods of procedure at the interment of the prisoners had been various, at times not very complimentary to a professedly Christian people. But more recently the custom had obtained of having prayer and remarks appropriate to the occasion, the men being arranged in the prison yard, after which they were to retire to their work. In this way we conducted our first funeral after my entrance. At the next, we observed this form: Had all things ready when the men were had eaten, say at twenty-five minutes past twelve, and then took them to the chapel for the usual prayer and remarks, which ended, we conducted them in file through the reception-room for leave-taking of their lifeless comrade, the body being there laid out with some little taste, and then they passed on to the shop. This method is chaste and appropriate, hinders nothing about the shop labor, and manifests due respect for the occasion.

The matter of funerals has ever been held as of great importance by all civilized nations. Nor is it any the less important to a well conducted prison than elsewhere. Proper funeral observances will tend to the good of the prisoners as well as to that of others, and help impress upon them the idea of their own mortal career and accountability. How much more like men they will cause the inmates to feel than would putting the body in a rough box and hauling it off the back way, in a cart, like a dead dog.

———————

27. *Educational and S. school summing up.* The year closed upon our educational efforts with a good measure of success, though of necessity limited in comparison with what ought to be accomplished by a like number in our public schools outside. For, it will be borne in mind, that all our pupils had to perform their daily tasks at manual labor from early morn till night; that their cells are not the most advantageous rooms for study; that what they obtained they had to gain in these pent up places, in the odds and ends of their time, as best they could. Then, again, we could have our school only when the guards could be spared from their common prison duties. Still, with all the drawbacks, a number of the inmates made commendable proficiency. They did what they could. They had become inspired with the idea of putting themselves earnestly to the task of cultivating their intellects and hearts, so far as they could, and thus be prepared, on leaving prison, for common business. Some had really waked up to what they had lost by their sinful courses, and now appeared determined to do their best, in the future, at making amends. Thus spurred on, they were diligent. And it was truly a pleasure to be permitted to help forward these minds, arousing, as they were, to a higher and better life. Sordid indeed must be that heart which would not fire up with energy for encouraging such to go on.

Some forty of the young were among those who were striving in this direction, a very few others of that class not possessing sufficient mental capacity for learning. Then others had obtained a good education previously, and chose to spend their time in reading from the library, except that some would wish a better knowledge of arithmetic, and perhaps other branches, when about to close their term.

We had been favored with a few interesting lectures from outside gentlemen, with three readings by lady elocutionists, and a number of drill exercises in singing. A gentleman also gave us a number of lessons in penmanship.

We had repaired the books of the library, added nearly two hundred volumes, obtained a new catalogue, two large blackboards for drill exercises in arithmetic, &c., a set of charts on penmanship, a set also of outline maps in geography, purchasing likewise such books or material as appeared needful to the school, expending in all $260.45, being allowed to use in this way the money gathered from the admission fees of visitors, all of which we did not use.

We endeavored to do what we could towards beginning what we confidently hoped would soon become an institution duly established by the State with all needed provision for security. The Sabbath school continued with unabated interest from the first, numbers varying but little, seldom falling below eighty, average, eighty-six.

28. *Religious success.* From my first day at the prison, the religious state had been encouraging, nothing to mar the interest transpiring. True, there had been no revival at any time, but a steady, healthful drawing in the right direction, that from which the most is ever to be hoped. A goodly number had, at different times, become professedly fixed in the determination to a thorough reform, while the others had, to appearance, largely lost their prejudice against religious truth; and entered more freely into conversation upon those subjects, many admitting the justness of their claims. And, taking all things together, our prospects had never appeared better than at the end of the year, indicating that, should our rulers possess wisdom enough to select the right man for warden, still more cheering results might be anticipated from subsequent efforts.

But we could not presume to judge correctly as to how much of this profession was well founded. That we had to leave for God to take care of. We had one important certainty, however, connected with this matter,—the certainty that all true good is found with just such surroundings as we had at the prison, the love of prayer, interest in God's Word, delight in attending meetings, desire for mental culture and a professed seeking for holiness; but not with the contrary, such as swearing, contentions, hatred of God's truth, and the like.

29. *Fourth of July at the prison.* The Fourth came with no new warden appointment. Therefore, the incumbent determined that he would celebrate this at the prison as his own yearnings prompted, and as it would be observed at some other prisons. Hence, at early morn, he announced to the men that he was about to give them a real Fourth, causing their hearts to leap for joy.

At 9 o'clock they met in the chapel for the reading of the Declaration of Independence, singing, &c., after which they marched into the prison yard, where were tables beautified by floral decorations and spread by fair hands, with picnic dainties, lemonade being prepared expressly for the prisoners. The blessing asked, the men having done ample justice to the good cheer, and the tables having been removed, speaking by a number of distinguished gentlemen from various towns followed. This ended and prayer offered, the sports followed as various as the different tastes could devise. Nothing rude, boisterous, insubordinate, or unkind appeared from any. One standing outside the walls would not have supposed, from anything heard, that a real, live Fourth was being so greatly enjoyed within. And probably the pleasures of the day were never more keenly felt anywhere, in prison or out. One and another would say, "This is the happiest day of my life." A somewhat large delegation of ladies and gentlemen from various parts of the State was present, who seemed delighted with the occasion. The female prisoners partook of their picnic dainties in their own room, but were permitted, with their attendants, to witness the yard scenes from the chapel windows. Everything passed off satisfactorily. The speaking was excellent, just fitted to the occasion, showing the need of laws and prisons, that those present were here for crimes, yet that they could reform, for which they should strive, that numerous willing hands were reached out for their encouragement and aid.

The time at length came for separating, when each man went to his cell with a cheer of heart which he had never carried there before. And this cheer long pervaded their minds, leading them to obey with greater alacrity. Nor did I hear of a case of a contrary character. They would afterwards often refer to the occasion as that *happy day.*

---

30. *The true principles of imprisoning and prison-managing on the idea of reform in the convict.* For the sake of brevity these principles are here set forth mainly by questions and answers.

What is the object of imprisoning?

This object is fourfold:

1. To prevent the criminal from injuring the public.

2. To deter from committing crime.

3. To punish the wrong doer.

4. To reform the erring.

On the first two of these two points there is no dispute, while some will not admit the third, and others proscribe the fourth. Let us, however, admit the four.

Who has the right to imprison and assign the terms and conditions to the imprisoned?

The State alone, or society organized in a body politic, has this right, and that is to be exercised by due process of law, in which exercise she is, first, in her legislative capacity, to point out clearly, by her enactments, for what a man shall be imprisoned, specify the terms of the imprisoning and the conditions to which the imprisoned shall be subjected; second, in her judicial capacity, assign the wrong doer his merited doom; and, third, in her executive capacity, to carry out in him the decisions she has made, no individual having a right to interfere with this in any way, except as specially authorized by State enactments.

Hence, the criminal, when standing at the bar and hearing the sentence of the judge, can understand exactly what lawfully and justly awaits him, provided that he demean himself uprightly in his new condition.

Suppose the sentence, in a given case, is this: "You are to be confined at hard labor in our State Prison for five years." In this all that can lawfully be inflicted upon the convict is involved. So say the judges themselves. Hence, should any man, or party of men, bring upon him additional infliction during that time, the imprisoned would, just so far, become the sufferer of a wrong, and those making that infliction would be the wrong doers. Let us, then, analyze this sentence and thus ascertain its elements.

Being confined in prison for the term, all admit, involves the idea that he is to enter those walls and not be permitted to pass out till his time is ended.

As the term, "hard labor," is not defined, it must be determined by the common custom of workmen at the same or similar business outside. So say the judges again. To illustrate: if ten hours constitute a day's work with these, so with the prisoners,—not twelve or fifteen. Again, if, in bedstead making, turning one hundred posts, in the one case, is required for a day, so in the other, not one hundred and fifty or two hundred. This laboring day after day, during the specified number of years, constitutes the "hard labor" in the meaning of the court.

The law assigns no further punishment to the imprisoned, if duly submissive to wholesome prison rules. But, should he be stubborn, refusing to perform his task, or obey the regulations generally, or should he rise in rebellion, of necessity discretion must be left with the officers to use such means, even to taking life, as shall be essential in bringing the delinquent to subordination. These means, however, may be limited by law, as they are to a great degree in our State, and are ever to be used as humanity dictates.

What rights does the State take from the criminal in imprisoning?

She takes from him the right to live and act outside of prison walls, to be a master to himself inside, and to receive his earnings as his own. These constitute the sum total. As he had used his liberty and the mastery of himself to the public damage, she justly steps in, deprives him of the one and takes upon herself the other, thereby assuming the guardianship over him during the specified time. She takes his earnings as a compensation, so far as they will go, for his damage and expense to community, and as an important element in his punishment. She becomes his guardian for the purpose of so educating him that, on going out, he shall live an upright, harmless life.

What rights remain to the imprisoned?

There is a wide range, a long list of these, which the State does not pretend to cut off or interfere with, such as the right to suitable food, clothing, lodging, ventilation, drainage, care in sickness or infirmity: in a word, to what will tend to corporeal vigor; the right to means for mental, moral and religious culture, or what will tend to the development in him of true manhood. If this is not so, which right is cut off or curtailed? and where is the law that does it?

What duties does the State take upon herself in thus imprisoning?

These are of two classes, one relating particularly to herself, and the other to the imprisoned.

Duty to herself is done, 1st, in protecting society from the crimes of the imprisoned, which she does by imprisoning; 2nd, in keeping the criminal diligently at work, thereby obtaining pecuniary compensation, so far as can be, for her trouble and expense on his account; 3d, in using all feasible efforts for rubbing off the rust of sin, washing away the corruption of iniquity, found in those taken in charge, and making of them true men,— good, industrious, honest, upright citizens.

The latter part is of the highest moment, far exceeding all considerations of mere dollars and cents, drawing as much real manhood as possible from the material put in her hands. If she takes one who is dangerous to society, and works in him an entire reform, she accomplishes a work in comparison with which gold and silver will weigh but little. Making men is the high mission of the prison, and the State can not be regarded as having performed anything like her whole duty, till she has used every feasible means to this great end.

The duty of the State to the prisoner is performed by securing to him what he needs in his corporeal, mental, moral and religious departments.

If she withholds in any of these, so far she becomes delinquent towards the imprisoned, a violator of his rights just as really as he had been a violator of others' rights when in his wild career of sinning.

More than this. In such withholding she becomes chargeable with real cruelty. For she has put the man in a state where he can not supply his own needs, and, if she neglects them, he must suffer. This is surely a grave matter, one which should be looked to with the utmost care;—a place where the State can afford to be highly generous rather than expose herself to a suspicion of such a wrong.

What are the proper means of reform?

Among these will be found, the State guardianship, the labor system, strict discipline, kind treatment, stimulating hope, mental, moral and religious culture.

The State guardianship will tend to form in the convict the habit of duly regarding the rights of others and of looking up, with respect, to wise and beneficent direction; the labor system, that of uniform industry, of profitably employing the time instead of in idle indulgencies; strict discipline, that of cheerful submission to wholesome rules, regardful of the principles of right. Kind treatment will tend to inspire the recipients with confidence in the sincerity of the reform efforts used, trust in the proffered friendship, and an assurance of success in struggles for good. Stimulating hope will rouse the better nature to action and secure confidence in overseers. Cultivating the intellect will prepare one intelligently to conduct himself in the affairs of life, and open to him sources of satisfaction far above those of his former life. Moral culture will arouse controlling ideas of the bounds of human rights, and the importance of observing them. The religious cultivation, having been made through deep conviction of sin, resulting in a hatred to wrong and a love for good, will lay a broad and deep foundation for a life of right.

Let these means be honestly and efficiently used, and they will most powerfully influence to ways of goodness. None of them can be spared. Each is a link in the chain which will be mighty to elevate the fallen. And if one can not be reformed by them, it is proof positive that he ought not to be at large.

What kind of prison officers are essential?

They should be of good moral character, ever setting proper examples before the prisoners, humanely disposed, capable of complete self-control, alive to efforts for reforming the inmates. Those more especially charged with the administration of affairs will need, in addition, to be good disciplinarians, studying the peculiarities of each and endeavoring to heal the weaknesses of mind.

The warden should possess great breadth of mind and force of character; be capable of bringing to his work large heart power; patient, yet decided; abounding with humane instincts, yet capable of using sterner means when essential; ever keeping wisdom at the helm, using true discretion, and be controlled by a strong desire for the highest good of all. He will be intent on studying how to address reform means to each with a view to the greatest success. At the same time he should look well to the true pecuniary interests of the institution.

The chaplain should be truly a man of God, enabled to bring large mental, moral and religious force to his duties, and alive, heart and soul, to the great work of raising up those under his care and presenting them to the world redeemed and saved.

31. *The commutation system.* This is a system established by legislative enactment a few years since; on condition of good behavior and a faithful performance of duty in one, to grant him a specified shortening in his term of sentence, and complete restoration to citizenship.

It was really interesting to witness the effect of this provision on the convicts, stimulating as it did their hope, and leading them to do the best they could to obtain this much coveted boon. The case of one will illustrate this feeling. He had been in the solitary, but did not seem to mind his sufferings there in the least. His great anxiety was whether he should lose his commutation. He suffered no little in mind in this respect. Indeed, every day gave us a clear exhibition of the influence this system had over the inmates' minds for good, helping the officers greatly in keeping order in their efforts at reform.

Now, if hope could be thus stimulated, and that to such great advantage, by this simple provision, what might not be accomplished by following more largely the same line of policy, that is, the hope-stimulating line?

32. *Chaplain's proposed attempt at tobacco reform.*

The chaplain made this proposition to the governor and council: "Put the prisoners on their option as to tobacco using with the condition that any who will disuse it, receive, once a month, or quarter, as the case may be, the amount thus saved in money, to be kept funded in the bank for him to receive, on certain conditions as to time, &c., after his release."

This proposition was made with at least four prominent objects in view. The first was to convert as many as could be from tobacco using; the second, to give an additional stimulus to hope among the prisoners; the third, to create an interest in the men in looking after money matters, a care for small items; and, fourth, to help them form the habit of saving and laying up.

This privilege was, of course, to be granted on condition of good behavior, and therefore as effective as could be toward prison order.

The proposer conceived that here was an element of great power for good to the prison and State. This forming a habit, in the former careless one, of looking particularly into the smallest items of money, with carefully saving and laying up, might work an entire revolution in more than one, leading them to habits of honest industry and thrift, an immense gain to the individual and the community.

But the rulers did not see fit to heed the proposal. If they had, no doubt quite a large number of the prisoners would have adopted the plan.

PART II.

Under the Punitive and Money-making System.

1. *Warden chosen, and new arrangements for the chaplain.* Some weeks of the new year had passed, when the warden's place was filled by the choice of J. C. Pillsbury, of Concord. Report said that the delay had been by reason of a division of sentiment on the case in the council chamber.

I directly waited on the new incumbent, at his office, to arrange for my duties. He seemed to feel that he had been put there for correcting important abuses that had grown up in the prison management, in what particular department I did not learn. But he laid out my work as follows:

"Chaplain, we will have the meetings held in the chapel as heretofore; that is, the males assemble Sabbath mornings at nine and enjoy the same exercises as usual, none else to be admitted except at my special invitation; Sabbath school continue Sabbath afternoons, and I will select such teachers as I think best. Wednesday evening prayer meetings to continue, I inviting in some of the religious men of the city to help carry them on, and not a prisoner be allowed to open his head in them. These fellows are here to be punished. They must not be called men, but criminals, for such they are."

Such in substance was my programme, on which this colloquy followed between myself and warden:

"Warden, you did not speak of admitting the female prisoners to the Sabbath worship in the chapel."

"No, I don't purpose to admit any females to that service."[1]

[1] I understood his objection to be, that the sight of a woman is demoralizing to a prisoner.

"But we can have a screen so arranged, that the women can not be seen by the men, though assembled as formerly, and I will be at the labor and expense of fitting it."

"No, I won't have a woman in the chapel."

"But do not the rules require the warden to assemble the females as well as males in the chapel Sabbath mornings for worship?"

"Oh, I call the women's work-room their chapel."

"But, if I am to hold a service with the women in their work-room after the chapel service, it will double my labors, and then not be as interesting and useful to them as if hearing the discourse with the speaker fresh and unfatigued."

"I don't ask you to hold a second service with the women, for giving them a sermon. Only go into their room any time in the week, some evening if more convenient, and offer prayer, and that will be all sufficient."

"How about commencing the school in the chapel?"

"Oh, I can't have anything to do with that, we are so tired, when night comes, with our other duties."

Thus matters were before me. What a cutting off! The question would be, "Is this cutting off a part of the proposed correction of prison abuses?" No secular school, no religious instruction of note to the female prisoners, and the screws put upon our prayer meeting so tightly as to render them of but little account to the prisoners.

As to the latter, I felt that, could the prisoners enjoy the privilege of taking part in them as previously, having only the warden, guards and myself present, it would be preferable to the new plan. This I proposed, to which the warden finally assented, and that from the fact, as I supposed, that it would rid him of so much outside attendance. This then was gained, though the other points remained immovably fixed.

I understood the warden to remark, "It is of no use for the chaplain to preach and labor with a hope of reforming these prisoners, for they can't be reformed." Then this expression, as of his saying, was told me,—"I will break up that Methodist camp meeting at the prison." What did the assertion mean? Was it a slur on our previous religious efforts? Or was it indicative of a shortening of our religious privileges? We had, at no time, any rush at our meetings, but few being admitted for want of room. A small number had attended and helped in our prayer meetings, more in the Sabbath school. All denominations were alike interested in the matter. Indeed, we had no denomination about it.

I brought the matter of the school and that of the females assembling in the chapel for worship to the notice of the governor, but the warden prevailed.

---

2. *Chaplain almost resolved to resign, but decides to continue and arrange his work.* Thus things put on so forbidding an aspect in every way, that it did not seem that I could accomplish any further good at the prison. True, I could draw my salary with almost nothing to do, the name go out that the institution had a chaplain, but being expected to drift on with the current, whichever way it might set, and at the end make up a glowing report of the prison doings and success, no matter what the facts might be. But my feelings rebelled at such an idea, and I thought, for a time, that I must

resign, and almost resolved upon the step. Then the question would arise, Is it right to leave those who have appeared so earnest to improve and reform? Something said, "No." Friends, too, learning my feelings on the subject, said decidedly that I must remain at the post.

I was in a hard place. There were the sentiments as uttered above, then the general spirit manifested, speaking louder than words, that "reform moves are all interlopers in prison, having no sort of business here." After looking the ground carefully over in my mind and thinking of all the connections, I saw that, by a greatly increased amount of labor, I could furnish the prisoners with a partial substitute for the chapel school. I had a right to visit them in the privacy of their cells, from morn till the hour for retiring in the evening. I could therefore hear their recitations there separately. No one could justly complain of this. Hence, I decided to remain, and laid out my work thus:—Sabbath, usual service with the men from nine to ten, and services in the women's work-room till eleven; then in the hospital with Jones, the murderer, and others as their cases allow, till twelve; Sabbath school services in the afternoon, besides visiting cells as much as possible; on other days, to spend noon and evenings visiting the cells in turn, hearing recitations and imparting instruction in the common school branches; besides changing the books Saturdays, as already, to change them at any other time when called for.

Thus I voluntarily undertook three times as much real hard work for the prisoners as my duty had previously demanded. The new order seemed to render it imperative, for I could do nothing in the educational line without it.

---

3. *Cells cleared of trinket-making and tracts.* The former warden was accustomed to distribute tracts among the prisoners. He also, by the assent of the government over him, had allowed the men, who desired it, to employ their otherwise idle moments by making small trinkets, as hair chains, paper folders, tooth-picks and small fancy boxes in imitation of what was done in certain other prisons, thereby, as was supposed, securing greater contentment and better order among the men. The new warden condemned all this as a great violation of good prison order. The candles, also, were condemned, and everything of the kind, with all the writing material or waste paper found in the cells, was removed, the spoils carefully measured, and the number of bushels sent the rounds of the papers as an evidence of the former abuses in this prison and of his labors to correct them.

I asked if the prisoners did not need to have the waste paper, at least, remain. "Oh," said he, "they will look out for that themselves." I could not then see how, but subsequently learned, much to the cost of the State.

---

4. *Necessity for the chaplain's undertaking what he did.* This necessity arose, not simply from the demands of the inmates for educational and reformatory means, but also from considerations of good prison order. True, the warden had the vanity to think he could control the men in whatever way he might undertake. The show of his cane would be sufficient for any emergency. But there was human nature in the prison as well as out, and, from the circumstances, it would be strange if it did not show itself. By taking away the prisoners' educational privileges, and the various articles referred to, much idle time would be left. How would this be employed? These men would naturally feel angry at being deprived of what they had enjoyed so long, and prized. This now unemployed time would give them ample opportunity for studying means of revenge, and some would no doubt turn their acumen in that direction. If a prisoner had any smartness, he would feel, from the circumstances, almost impelled to give vent to mischief, and thereby make as much trouble as possible.

But, could I step in, and, by dint of effort, keep those minds agreeably occupied, I should do so much towards helping the warden to the desired subordination and order. No previous time in my prison experience seemed to demand so great efforts in that direction as now. Hence, duty appeared calling me to step forward, as I did.

---

5. *New phase at the prison, and the chaplain's efforts.* The first Sabbath morning came for chapel worship under the new order, and a sadder appearing company I never met, their countenances being expressive of anxiety and gloom commingled. The singing dragged, the instrument standing voiceless, as the one who had usually made it speak, was of the sex here proscribed, and the warden had not found another to take her place. It was hard preaching, for these once earnest hearers seemed to have hearts too full for hearing. But I endeavored to give words of hope, and to direct their minds to a heavenly Father who will ever carry his trusting children through the scenes they are called to pass. Of course I could make no allusion to present circumstances, or appear to recognize any change in the surroundings; but somehow I could not call the hearers "criminals." I pursued the usual course, addressing them as *men*, or *friends*, or perhaps *brothers*, for I was occasionally guilty of all that; but the word "criminal" never hung on my lips when addressing the inmates on subjects of improvement. In my view, such a course would have been like attempting

to light a fire by applying the match with one hand and dashing on water with the other.

At the close of our services, as the warden, in his peculiar way, was giving some of his orders, I could see the crimson flush on more than one cheek, indicative of the feelings stirred within, the character of which I could only conjecture. One of his assertions was, as I understood it, thus: "I am warden here now. The days of bouquets and flowers are played out here," and more in the same vein.

In the women's room the countenances were not so anxious. They rather liked this part of the change, for it would free them from the task of preparing, Sabbath mornings, to appear in public. Still, anxiety was not entirely wanting. Sabbath school was this day omitted, as the warden had not obtained his corps of teachers.

On going my rounds for private counsel to the men in their cells, I found, in most cases, gloom and discouragement, they having generally heard of the warden's disbelief in their reform. It was really wonderful to witness the change a few days had wrought in the moral aspect of the prison. A frost in June would not make a greater change on the face of nature. I could but ask myself, "Why are things thus?" "At what are our rulers aiming?"

I went to each with all the cheer I could, exhorting them not to indulge in these downcast feelings, but to look upward with hope, and gave them the assurance that their educational privileges, as well as religious, would be continued, only with some change in their application, and pointed out in brief the manner, saying that each could advance in study as rapidly as in his power.

If any referred to their cell amusements being taken away, I met them with the remark,—"Don't trouble about that. You shall be furnished with all the books you can read and study, and I will hear your recitations. In this way, your time can be pleasantly and profitably occupied, perhaps making you the gainers." A few of these former trinket workers became more interested in their studies, but the most could not, by reason of their sight, thus being left to endure their privation as best they could.

When one would refer to his discouragement on account of the warden's disbelief in reform, I would meet him thus, "You are to look only to yourself and your God in this matter. What a fellow mortal believes or disbelieves concerning you is of no account. You have the power to go on in the right and be a good man. I know you have, and others who are good and true, men upon whose views we can all rely, also know it. What matter if the warden does think as you suppose? It is only his opinion. He wishes you to do well, and will be glad if you succeed in the right. But, should you turn back, it will confirm his views that you can not reform. You will meet with harder things than this in life, yet must not think of yielding the struggle, let what will arise."

These efforts tended materially to lift the cloud from the prisoners' minds, and give them more hope. It really gladdened the hearts of many to learn that the privileges, which they had come to love so well and esteem so highly, were still to be theirs.

---

6. *S. school commences.* The next Sabbath the S. S. was resumed. Nearly the usual number were present. A few Christian gentlemen from the city were teachers, a sufficient number to guard each prisoner and see that nothing contraband passed. These were good men, some having long been laborers in the school. On the whole, things appeared more encouraging than on the Sabbath previous. That frosty appearance had in a measure departed, though it was by no means wholly gone.

---

7. *The warden's views considered.* The idea that "prisoners can not be reformed" is contrary to Scripture, history, and experience. The former gives the assurance that the vilest, the chief of sinners, those whose sins are as scarlet or crimson, may be saved. Then history deals in facts where such have been radically reformed, and have become good men. Some who were once in prison are now upright, industrious citizens. Hence, the assertion shows lack of confidence in Scripture assurances and historical knowledge.

But one asks, "Do you think it possible to reform all, or a large proportion of prisoners?" We can assume it of those here as of the world in general. Whether out of or in prison, we are to sow the seed, and some will germinate. We must work, use all right appliances, and leave the event with God, not knowing "which shall prosper, this or that."

Again, the objection comes: "Prisoners will be often hypocritical, profess goodness from sinister motives, pretending to have reformed for a time, and then become as bad as ever."

Admit all this. But are not just such traits found in the world all about us? Where are there more wicked wretches than some outside the prison, who have "put on the livery of heaven to serve the devil in?" What meaner men inhabit God's earth than some who have succeeded in working themselves into the church, and can boast of coming to the communion regularly? How many profess and fall away on every hand, yes, sink deeper in corruption than before! The fact is, this pretended argument to the disadvantage of the prisoner is all a sham.

The prison, if rightly conducted, possesses certain means of reform, which can not be had outside. To illustrate: Here is a young man, who has never entered a school-house, or a place of worship, but has spent his time with vicious companions and in vicious habits. He falls into prison, where his home is a cell and silence his constant companion. Here he is removed from his former surroundings and opportunities for sinful indulgence. The loneliness and tedium of his condition soon become unendurable. He must, in some way, have relief. But no means lie within his reach except those connected with reform appliances. To these he is forced, by the pressure of his nature, to resort, simply for self-gratification, which he can find in hearing the human voice and in the connected exercises. He hears truth which he had never heard before, but which is permitted to fall on his mind with its full weight. He is thus led to reflect, repents of his sins, and becomes really a reformed man, a brand plucked from the burning.

The tendency of things, then, in a properly conducted prison, *is* reformatory. Therefore, let ours be managed on that principle, and all in our State, worthy of such a place, be there assigned for the requisite time, and, no doubt, one good, devoted, wide-awake man could do them more good than they now receive from all the religious means and labors outside put together.

"The sight of a woman is demoralizing to a prisoner." The reader will readily understand in what respect. If this be true, what a demoralized class must be our grown up, unmarried sons, our bachelors and widowers, with women constantly in sight. Then how wickedly does the warden himself proceed in taking certain of his men among the women to work; and in permitting women and girls dressed up in their finery to perambulate freely about the shops and buildings in sight of the men.

"But," it is answered, "the men are not allowed to look at visitors." True, but not being allowed is one thing, and not looking is quite another. If any man can make himself believe that, when a woman is conducted right into the presence of a prisoner, he will not obtain a sight of her, he possesses more credulity than falls to the common lot of men. The fact is, visitors about the shops are seen by the prisoners and thought of and talked about by them, no matter who pretends to the contrary. Every one knows this, who knows anything of a prison, let him say what he will. Then why select one spot, the chapel on the Sabbath, as a place where the sight of a woman is to be branded as a most polluting sin, and no objection raised to her being seen elsewhere almost daily and hourly? Consistency is a jewel.

If the sight of a woman is so demoralizing to a man confined in prison, how demoralized must he speedily become on leaving and meeting them everywhere! And what sinners prison managers in numerous other States have become through admitting women to moral labors in their institutions! What egregious sinning on the part of that State which employs a woman as chaplain of its prison, and she permitted to go freely from cell to cell in her ministrations of mercy!

In the army, in hospitals, or whatever place men are found needy and dependent, true women are freely admitted as ministering angels, with no thought of demoralization. Yes, the world lauds the heroism and devotion of many of these in poetry and song.

So far as I could learn, the influence of the women in the chapel did not produce the effect alleged. I inquired of some on this point, at the time of their leaving, and solicited the real truth. Take the answer of an intelligent young man, one whom I have no doubt is sincere and reliable,—"The influence on my feelings were not in a wrong direction, but wholly to the contrary. I should have been ashamed of myself at indulging an impure thought towards that lady under whose care I was so long in the Sabbath school. I rather felt humbled and filled with gratitude, that she should condescend to take me, a poor, wicked prisoner, not able to read or write, and labor so patiently and persistently to help me to what I now am, redeemed, I trust, and made a different man, largely through her labors. They were her words of hope and assurance which first stimulated me with the idea of an earnest effort to rise from what I was."

The fact is, some men have their passions and will think, whether seeing any of the other sex or not; and more or less are inclined to deeds of wrong. But, in the opinion of our best minds, the true course to pursue is, to admit judicious ladies, those of character and influence, to help in labors of reform.

"Motives of safety required the cell clearing." This was the pretended reason, but could not have been the real one, according to the warden's own words. One day, in passing along the cells with company, he remarked, "Gentlemen, vigilance, vigilance, is the only safety here! Lock me in one of those cells, and I would walk out in half an hour. There is no safety in this prison but in the watchfulness of the guard." This being true, the small articles which the warden found in the cells could make no difference in regard to safety, therefore, their removal must have been from other motives.

8. *Chaplain's restrictions.* These were not given at once and in detail, but were learned by experience. One afternoon, the prisoners being in the shop, I took the key, as sometimes before, when needful, to enter the chapel by the south door, where there could have been no possible danger had the men

been passing to their cells; having gone a few steps, I heard the voice of the warden calling out, sternly,—"Chaplain, here, what are you doing with that key?" I informed him, and received the reply, "Bring that key right back. You must not touch a key." Quietly obeying, I returned the article and never touched it again, thinking, "If he will speak out to me as an irritated father to a vexatious boy, what can be expected for the prisoners?" He had a perfect right to require me not to use the key, and I had a right to a gentlemanly treatment. I uttered not a word, though I could not help thinking. Afterwards when needing to enter the chapel, I must ask a guard, perhaps a mere boy, to go and unlock and lock the door for me, which seemed really ludicrous. Shortly after, I heard the warden speaking of his enormous burden in the line of watchfulness,—"I have to watch not only the prisoners to keep them right, but also the workmen, overseers, guards, steward, physician and chaplain."

At another time I asked him to change the position of a class in the Sabbath school to accommodate the singing, and received an answer not so insolent in tone as before, but, with the connected circumstances, equally clear for me to understand that I must propose no move, make no suggestion whatever about the school, leaving everything in that line to him. I could open and close the school and hear also those not otherwise provided for.

Again, finding a man in his cell with no lesson, he having broken his glasses, I passed them to the deputy to be repaired. Days passed, and no glasses were returned. Meeting the warden, I alluded to the matter. He replied, "Chaplain, I would have you know that when a man needs anything, he must speak of it to the deputy or to me. You have no business with these things." To my inquiry, "Am I to understand that now, after speaking to you about the glasses, and putting them in the deputy's hands, the man must speak to one of you himself, before they can be returned?" he answered, "Certainly." Hence, on my next round, I said to the owner, "Please speak to the warden or deputy about your glasses, and they will return them, probably, all right," not giving him the least hint as to how matters really stood, though I could but think, "Here is red-tapeism with a vengeance; not permitted to speak of anything in my own department." Waiting for a time, and thinking that neither law nor gospel would object to my lending him my own, this I did, which he used until liberated. True, after some weeks, glasses were brought him, in which, however, he could not see.

Thus I was effectively taught my bounds, to touch nothing about the prison but my books, to suggest no change any way, and to bring nothing to the warden, or deputy, about a prisoner, which bounds I was ever careful to observe.

There was an attendant rule to this red tapeism, as I understood it, that bore hard on the prisoners,—that one must ask for a thing but once. Some would ask me to help them to an article, when I would say, "You must go with that to the deputy, or warden." They replied, "I have, with the promise of it, but it does not come." Or, perhaps, "I ventured to ask the second time, and received the stern reply, 'Don't you ever mention that to me, again.'"

A forlorn condition this,—the State placing her wards helplessly under a man who is not to be reminded of a request, which had slipped his mind, perhaps, through the multiplicity of business. Surely, such a man should be very considerate and particularly careful about attending to the needs of his dependents.

The lessons taught me, the spirit manifested with all the surroundings, gave me to understand that I must walk in everything with the utmost circumspection or be mercilessly dealt with. True, I had ever labored to do all things in my prison management just as I should, ever acting with an eye single to the best prison order; but circumstances now evidently demanded of me a double care, that my every step should not only be right but appear right, and no shadow of grounds for complaint be any way found.

---

9. *Prisoners' Aid Association.* In the spring of '70, a company of ladies and gentlemen organized under the N. H. statutes into a corporate body by this title, to hold its annual meeting in the city of Concord, the second Tuesday of each June, the avowed purpose being to aid the discharged convicts by proper advice, and help them to places of labor without delay, where they may enjoy the needed society privileges, guardian care, and a general influence in favor of their best success, paying for them such small bills as may be necessary for this purpose.

The legislature of that season voted the Association three hundred dollars, to aid it in its benevolent work, I being appointed agent for that purpose.

---

10. *Complaint of prison hunger.* Late in the summer, a man, leaving prison, complained that the prison living was not as good as that of the past year, the rations being poorer in quality, and less in quantity; that, at times, he had really so suffered with hunger that he could not sleep at night. I questioned him carefully, and he appeared honest in his statements, still, this being the first I had heard of such complaints, I would not form an opinion from this assertion, for he might be telling the story to injure the warden. But he gave this account here and there in the city, so that it was

circulated widely. A lady, as she asserts, asked the prison physician if the rations had been reduced, and he replied that they had to some extent.

The reader will understand, that while I had no right to converse with the inmates about their food, and other like subjects, and did not while they were there confined, yet, when they had been released and become citizens, nothing lay in the way of my freely conversing with them on all matters as with others.

---

11. *Chaplain's object in hearing from released prisoners and others.* This object was purely to learn the true working of things, and thus be prepared to conduct myself understandingly in all my prison duties. I had served a year under a certain system, studying with care its workings and effects on the men, and had now entered service under one that seemed measurably different, the operations of which, also, I ought to comprehend. I would, therefore, listen to those who were released, study what might come to hand in this way, from personal observation in official intercourse, or from reading authors, and use whatever hints were gained, to the best advantage.

But one says, "Those fellows from prison will lie." Grant that. Grant that here are twenty of the greatest liars in the State about to leave prison in course. But they have no opportunity, while there, for mutual conversation and planning a particular story to tell on leaving; nor do they even know of having an opportunity, outside, to talk with me or any particular one. They severally leave their confinement, each giving account of his experience, which I put down. On looking these carefully over, a line of substantial agreement is found running through the whole. We cut off whatever, in any, seems essentially deviating. But every judge in the land will admit that that general line contains the truth.

This illustrates my course of procedure, and my grounds for believing prisoners. Then, again, where one voluntarily, without my alluding to the matter, gave me an account of a subject, part of which I knew to be correct, I had every reason to believe the remainder was correct, also.

---

12. *B. and E.'s request, and the connected abuse.* These men, before spoken of, had become much interested in the moral and religious instruction given by those lady friends, Mrs. E. and D., to whom they had been introduced in the manner already pointed out. Request was extended to the warden that they might have the privilege of corresponding, but he peremptorily refused; why, none could conceive, though some would contend that the reason must be found in the vindictive, for the correspondence was to go through the usual channel and be open to his own inspection, that, had

anything objectionable appeared, he could have suppressed it, or stopped the whole correspondence. Those ladies were capable of writing excellent letters, letters by which any right-minded man would be benefited, the warden himself being judge. I have no doubt that should he meet some of their productions, unaware of their authorship, he would pronounce them of a superior character, and say that "the more of such writings the prisoners can have to read, the better." The men did not ask for a personal interview with those ladies, but simply their words; words which would stimulate them to higher aims, and enable them the better to endure the trials of prison life. The warden possessed the right, if he chose to exercise it, to interdict this correspondence wholly. But I protest that he had no right to defame those ladies, villify their character, and speak of them to those men, and to prison visitors from whatever part of the country, as "those mean women," "those base women," "those low women."

As before stated, they were ladies with the best of characters,—earnest Christian workers, invited to the interviews by the mother and warden, and always having them in the presence of the latter. These visits were for a most praiseworthy purpose. If it is ever right for a high-minded, upright, Christian lady to call on the fallen for the purpose of helping them rise from their degraded state, those ladies are to be commended for the efforts they made in behalf of those prisoners.

But these men were forced to suffer no little abuse in relation to those visits,—not by fellow prisoners, understand. They were taunted in the most vulgar, low, indecent language. One day it went so far with one, that he became aroused beyond endurance, and replied, "You know that is a —— —— lie," filling the blanks with two most profane words as qualifying "lie." On my next round he told me his trouble, what he had said, how he was being assailed, and that he probably must relinquish all idea of being any better. I replied, "Don't you understand what all this is for? It is the work of Satan, for your destruction. They would excite you to anger and turn you to your old life of profanity and wickedness; if possible, sink you as low as ever. You have but one course to pursue, and that is, to pay no attention to them. Let them say what they may, give it no more notice than the idle wind. Be sure and not suffer yourself to become irritated, or say a word in return, and they will probably leave you. But if not, endure it patiently, and pray God to forgive what you have done amiss and keep you in the future." In following this course, he succeeded better.

13. *Alleged prison conspiracy.* The next one who left made no complaint of the living, he had been sick and received all the food he desired, but he asserted that trouble was brewing at the prison; that they were planning to kill the

warden. I made light of the idea as something of his own conjuring up, that the prisoners would not undertake such a matter. Finally he said, "Mark my words, Chaplain, there will be blood shed over there within a month." This man was a singular genius, and I thought he might wish to start such a story to nettle the warden. Besides, they were as vigilant as possible at the prison, and the inmates would find them alert, should they attempt to rise. From all considerations, I thought it not worth while to speak of the case to any. Still, it would do no harm to prepare and deliver a discourse from the text, "Vengeance is mine and I will repay, saith the Lord," designing to show the impolicy of attempting to take vengeance into one's own hands, and that vengeance should be left for God to repay.—The discourse was given, and things passed on as usual, no signs of an outbreak appearing, and I finally gave the matter up as one of the man's imaginings.

But, the next spring, one of the prisoners, when leaving, alluded to a combination of a number, the year previous, and said considerable preparation for the work had been made, but after hearing that Sabbath's discourse, so many abandoned the project that the leaders had to relinquish their effort. This was repeated in substance by another. Hence, after all, it appeared that what the first man said may have been true, and that, possibly, my poor labors may have been of service to the warden, perhaps saved his life. Certainly, I did what I could.

---

14. *National Prison Reform Congress.* In October this body assembled for deliberation at Cincinnati, O., it being the first gathering of the kind. Delegates were present from a large number of the United States, also from the British Provinces and South America, but I was the only one from New Hampshire. The great, central ideas pervading the body were the finding of the best method of prison management and how to introduce this to general and uniform use. All the subjects so earnestly grappled there, would hinge around these. The field was somewhat widely examined and much discussion awakened,—discussion earnest, though courteous. The religious element largely predominated, and great harmony prevailed. True, an atheist attempted to throw in a firebrand by making a cat's paw of the Jew, but wholly failed, not exciting a single remark in reply. A U. S. judge was present, several State judges, a number of governors and ex-governors, lawyers, clergymen, philanthropists in private life and prison officials, showing that the move had taken strong hold of that class, especially, which will push it forward.

Those prison officers present who had ever persisted in the knock-down argument of former generations, were moved forward many years. I thought of N. H., and wished that some of her fossils could have been present and become vitalized. What a blessing it would be to the State!

The points considered and settled, so far as that body could settle them, were drawn up in thirty-seven articles for general distribution. One set forth reform as the paramount object of imprisoning, another, that kindness and humane treatment should prevail in all prison management. But the reader would be well repaid by sending for the "Transactions" of the body, a work of some seven hundred pages, and carefully perusing it. It will cost three dollars, and is to be had of Rev. E. C. Wines, D. D., No. 48 Bible House, N. Y.

The convention was not only pleasant in itself, but also in its surroundings. The city extended it a welcome through an excellent address by the Mayor, inviting the body to a dinner and visit to its public institutions and places of interest, and furnishing coaches to convey the members. It also provided a convenient hall for the sittings. A number of the city societies also invited us to their gatherings.

This Congress arranged for its perpetuity by becoming an incorporate body in some State and holding its sessions biennially. This has been consummated by obtaining a charter in the State, of New York, Ex-Governor Seymour being President, and Rev. E. C. Wines, Cor. Secretary. It also took incipient steps for an international congress to be held in London, England, choosing Dr. Wines also as Commissioner to carry the proposal into effect.

---

15. *Money-making and punishing, the paramount objects in our prison management.* For a time, I had been at a loss about the real objects of the present manner of conducting prison affairs, but it had become evident that money-making and punishing were those objects. To the former the prison agent and warden seemed bending their united energies as best they could. They would make a better exhibit of gains than ever before, a great compliment to the one as a financier and to the other as a prison manager. To this end, they would bend their efforts in purchasing and disbursing, having, to appearance, left all moral considerations out of the question. I was informed that the warden said, "I will clear five thousand for the State this year, if I have to use up every man in doing it."

Then punishment was to go hand and hand with this gain making, as the warden was reported as saying to the prisoners, "I mean to use you so that you will not wish to come back," meaning, of course, usage beyond what the law and courts contemplate.

---

16. *Waste paper in the cells.* The warden's clearing the cells of this has been spoken of and a connected point, I could not comprehend. In the course of months, all became clear. The fly leaves of the library books, and some of the other leaves, were gone, which told the story.

Had it been the season previous, I should have detected the matter sooner and stopped it, but now I could not. Then, when the general repairs were made to the library, I found that many of the books had been lost, to avoid which, in the future, I adopted a new method here, of charging every book let out and crediting its return. But this required no little increase of labor, in consideration of which, the former warden furnished me an assistant in the book charging and book inspection. On two Saturdays after the new warden came in, I asked for the usual assistance, but, from what passed, I found it best to ask no more for aid, and decided to do the work myself as best I could, continuing the account keeping, however, though with no possibility of the former inspection.

I supposed the warden desired me to curtail the book changing, for, passing the table one day, loaded with books ready for the hall, he said, "Why, chaplain, the men don't need all those books." My reply was, "They called for them all." "Well," said he, "they can not read them;" meaning, as I took it, that I should not furnish so many. But I was particular to give out all called for, a more generous supply, it is true, than formerly, for the purpose of keeping the men engaged and quiet under his peculiar management.

———————

17. *Defective beds and bedding.* Those iron cross bars to the bedsteads cut the straw, hence the former warden made it a point to refill the beds once a quarter, but the latter filled them perhaps once in six months. Indeed, some would be neglected till nothing could be found in the bed-tick but a mass of chaff-like substance to which the straw had been reduced, thus leaving the occupant with little besides the bare slats on which to sleep. Men would at times complain that, from that cause, they could obtain but little rest at night, and were in the morning so sore and stiff that, for a time, it would be difficult for them to move.

During the fall they did not attend to the needed general mending and refitting of the old comfortables and bedspreads, though some were ragged and filthy, or worn so thin as to be but little better than so many strainers. The cells on the lower floor were exceptions. But few of these were used. All the beds were kept well filled; having good spreads, sheets and pillow cases. They made a few comfortables for these unused beds, and indeed all these cells were kept in good order, nicely dusted, &c., and the doors were set open by day for visitors to admire. Hence, I would hear them crying out, "How nice you keep things here! What comfortable beds! How neat!" I would think within,—not aloud, for that would not do,—"O that you could look into those higher up. You might cry out, 'Pig's nests!'" These new comfortables were made only two-thirds the usual width, answering well for an unused bed. Still I did occasionally see one on a bed in use.

As I was informed, a gentleman from outside had a view of those upper cells, the warden saying, in excuse for their condition, that he put the more slovenly in them, those who would not keep their cells in order. But the real truth of that matter is, some of the neatest men occupied those higher cells intermingled with those not so neat, the men being located as to their cells according to their position at work in the shop.

The sheets were so scarce as not to afford a full change for washing, requiring some to use dirty sheets, for a time, from another's bed, though less dirty than their own.

The former warden had been aiming to have, so far as could be, two suits to a man, a common, every day suit, and one better for Sabbaths, &c., it being thought that this would tend to refine and elevate the prisoners. Hence, he left them with a generous supply, well fitted up. But it would need more or less renewing and refitting in the fall, which it did not receive, but was made to answer by patching. Hence, patched and ragged clothes would be of no uncommon occurrence, as all became thin from long wear, the under-clothing, especially, much needing repairs and renewing.

The main seamstress left the next April, and told me that after this warden came in, up to that time, they had made one new suit and one other jacket, the new suit for the Newmarket murderer, who was too large for any they had on hand.

***

18. *Cracked wheat dinner.* In the fall, there was much complaint among the prisoners that their Monday dinner, which they formerly prized as the best in the week, had been changed to a dish that few liked and many could not eat. It was boiled cracked wheat with a little meat chopped in, no sauce or other relish upon it. I mentioned the case to the doctor, who said, "They purchased a quantity of potatoes, half a peck of which I took to my house and cooked, finding only one or two, among the whole, fit to put into the human stomach. Hence, I looked over my army dietary, found the cracked wheat answered a good purpose, and proposed it here." The potatoes were watery.

My attention had now been so loudly called to the prison living by the complaints of those liberated, that I determined to observe for myself, so far as opportunity might offer, keeping my own counsel in this as in all other matters, that I might be the better prepared to judge of the truthfulness of their stories. Notwithstanding the cracked wheat, those potatoes were set before them. If not at this meal, they were at others, but largely returned untouched. The substituted dish would also be regularly returned by a large number. But why purchase these potatoes "not fit to be put into the human stomach"? True, many such were in the market, but there were good ones, too, though costing more money. Families in the city found no difficulty about obtaining a good article. These, of course, came at a low figure, favoring here, as did everything else, this money-making idea.

----

19. *Bad fish, &c.* In the fall, the agent informed me, he had made for the state what he considered a great bargain, in the purchase of between one and two tons of fish. He said, "I found this in the hands of a man who had attempted to prepare it after a certain patent, but had, some way, missed his point and could not sell it. Had he succeeded, it would have brought thirteen cents a pound. He offered it to me for three. I took some to the prison, and they said that they could use it, hence, I purchased the whole." He further remarked, that the article was covered with a reddish mold. This, I was informed, is a sign of decay in fish. He also alluded to the great reduction in price he obtained on his prison supply of molasses.—It should be understood that this is used at all times in prison, on bread, as a substitute for butter.

After this, those leaving prison had these additional grounds for complaint. They complained, also, that the tobacco was very bad in quality and scant in quantity, the very cheapest article. One said that the scent of the fish carried into his cell at noon, would not be gone on his return at night. A woman, a waiter on the prison family table at the time of the purchase of the fish, informed me of its ordeal there. Nothing having been said to call her attention that way, but of her own accord, she said, "They bought a lot of bad fish at the prison, and the warden would have some prepared for the family table. He ate of it himself, pronounced it good, and wished the deputy, guards and overseers to eat of it also; but they would not, though he offered one a dollar, if he would." Now, as this woman's story was true as to the purchasing of the article and its quality, we have every reason to suppose it true in other respects. One said of the cracked wheat, that he could not force it down; it would made him sick; that others about him were similarly effected in their attempts to eat of the article.

----

20. *Prison suffering from cold during the winter of '70 & '71.* From the character of the food and clothing, the one not fitted to generate the needed supply of warmth within, nor the other to give the requisite protection without,

the men, to pass the rigors of winter, especially such as that of '70 and '71, without suffering, would need an unusually generous supply of artificial heat in the hall and shop. But instead of that, they were forced to experience the biting reality of a cutting off here, too, the place being too important for money-saving not to be used. True, it would cost something, but the custom had been to keep the hall comfortable through cold weather. Early in the morning they would let the steam into the shop and have that warm when the men were ready to commence their work, and keep it so during the day. But a different policy had now been adopted.

The present fall had nearly passed and no steam had been admitted into these apartments at all, the cook-room and reception-room drawing from the waste steam and engine boilers. People outside had long been using fires constantly and freely. At length, a remark of the warden to company, revealed the theory he was pretending then to act upon. The temperature, at the time, was low in the hall, and some excuse evidently appeared to be needful. The remark was this: "I have not let the heat into this hall yet, for I think it best to do with that as people ought to do with regard to under-clothing, keep it off as late as possible in the fall, and it will do them more good in winter. And, besides, these stones were so heated up last summer, that they have not become fully cooled yet." "What a happy thing for the men, when shivering here, as they do with the cold, could they find some of that stored up heat," thought I. But they could not, and hence were called to experience a severe foretaste of what lay before them in still colder weather.

But at length the hall boiler was set to work, bringing warmth and gladness to the men. And how cheerful and thankful they appeared! It was really a comfort to witness their relief, as I went about my labors. This, however, was only for a few days, for a great drain was being made upon the wood-pile, incurring too large a draft upon the prison gains to be endured. The boiler was stopped, to be run no more for the winter, dependence for heat here, in the future, to be had upon the steam, waste or otherwise, from the shop boilers, and even that but sparingly.

The custom adopted was to let the steam into the hall pipes just before the men were to enter from work, could it be spared from the cook room, sometimes perhaps ten or fifteen minutes, and then turned off early in the evening. That, of course, could do but little good, and hence a really keen atmosphere would at times be felt in the hall, causing much suffering there. How great the contrast to that of the office, which was so warm that the occupants would be at work with coats off; or the reception room, where I would perspire in labor upon my books, and enter the hall to find it much like going directly out of doors. Twice I thus took severe colds, after which I usually wore an overcoat to this apartment during the severe weather.

When those keen nights came on, some of the men would beg of me most pitiably for more bed-clothing, asserting that they were suffering alive, it sometimes seeming as though they must perish. I could only direct them to the warden or deputy for this. One said, "I have asked the warden, who replied, 'You have more clothes on your bed now than you ever had at home,' and passed on." This man had one of those strainer-like spreads and another somewhat thicker, doing well enough for early fall, but not a suitable protection in such weather. Another said, "Suffering so with cold that sleep is out of the question, I arise, dress, wrap about me what bedding I have, and walk my cell for the night, in that way keeping as much as possible from suffering."

The first evening after hearing these earnest pleadings, I met the steward and asked if he could not furnish these men with more clothing, with the answer, "The fact is, these fellows are down on the warden and determined to keep asking for something." To which I replied, "They very much need more clothing, and must greatly suffer without it." He answered, "Oh, our soldiers in the army suffered a great deal more than these fellows do, and you thought nothing of that. The fact is, you have too much feeling for these men." I left, with the remark, "I think we ought to have some humanity about us."

Thus was the attempt made to plaster over this outrageous cruelty by alluding to events which could not, in the very nature of things, be avoided. I say outrageous, for there was bedding enough on those unused beds, such as it was, to have done something towards relieving this suffering, but they would not permit them to have that. Then New Hampshire possessed wood and water enough to keep that room comfortable. If the boiler needed repairs, workmen for doing that were at hand; or, if it needed renewing, that could have been easily accomplished. Or they might have set large coal stoves at work.

But all did not thus lack for bedding. Some, by oversight or favoritism, had a surplus, using comfortables as a substitute for straw. A man thus supplied sent one of his extra number to the relief of another, as this sufferer subsequently informed me.

On those cold Sabbaths, the men would wrap their bed clothing about them, sit reclining on their beds, and read. The warden would not allow the shop to be warmed at all. Those cold mornings and those cold days it was excessively severe. The overseers had to bundle up with extra clothing to prevent suffering. One day the men had become too much benumbed to work and the foreman stopped the machinery, let the steam into the shop, thawed them out, and then went on again.

Having heard the warden say that the water in their reservoir was low, causing him fears of its failing, and meeting the governor, to his inquiry about our prison affairs, I alluded to the coldness there and the warden's remark, and received the reply, "Why, it won't do to let the men suffer with the cold. If need be, he must haul water from the river," and he sent the warden a letter to that import. But no water was hauled, and no amelioration had from the cold till, at length, when the severest weather had nearly passed, one of the council visited the prison and ordered a coal stove to be placed in a part of the hall, which gave a measure of alleviation. Still the men continued to suffer more or less till the change of weather brought the desired relief. They will ever look back to that as a suffering winter.

The women probably suffered less from the cold than the men. Still, they were put on short allowance and were obliged to carry their wood up those two flights of stairs, taking it from quite a distance out of doors, some of it being very large. One of those cold Sabbaths, entering their room for meeting, I found it so cold as to endanger my health, and, not then knowing the restrictions, I attempted to kindle the fire, but found only a few coals in the stove and one large stick in the box, which I placed with the coals, but with little effect. We had short exercises, and I left them to endure this temperature as best they could.

The women would watch the warden and steal a little extra, when he stepped out of sight, thus occasionally enjoying the genial warmth; if detected, however, to receive a gratuitous lecture. Finding, at length, that this extra labor was preying sadly upon their health, and having repeatedly importuned the warden for relief in vain, they turned to his wife, who informed him of the real effects being produced, with the assurance that the continuance of this drudgery would shortly bring the sufferers upon beds of sickness, requiring him to hire outside help, to care for them and perform the tasks in which they had failed. This gained the victory, but not till great injury had been done to the victims, the strongest, on whom the burden of carrying the largest had fallen, having thus laid the foundation for weeks of severe sickness and leaving prison an invalid, though previously a robust, healthy woman.

21. *Lighting the hall.* The candles having been banished from the cells, the gas was set at work when evening arrived. But at length the men began to complain of the great strain upon their eyes, and finally of failing sight. Advising them to lay aside reading and study till relief could be had, I reported the matter to the doctor, and, I think, to the governor. Not seeing any remedial move, however, I resorted to the dollar and cent

consideration, and, on investigating, found that, while they were paying $50 per month for that poor light, I could light the cells with candles, three a week to a cell, probably for fourteen dollars. I offered to obligate myself to do it for twenty, and receive only the actual cost whatever it might be below; also to see that no additional trouble came from the melting of the tallow. This argument prevailed, and the warden was ordered to furnish the candles, though he allowed only two a week to a cell. Some of the men were amused and some provoked at the manner of his announcing the change: "I have concluded to furnish you with candles, for your good, and hope you will use them as such;" for, it seems, they knew by what means the relief had come, though how I never understood.

---

22. *The aid of the Association to released prisoners, and warden's course.* The Association proved itself as advantageous to the discharged prisoners as the most ardent laborer for its establishment had hoped. An unusually large number left prison the present year, forty-two. In warm weather many would not require pecuniary aid, while others would. Thus, one required cooper's tools to the amount of six and one-half dollars; another, a railroad pass to Ohio, for twelve dollars; a third, a pass to Wisconsin, at thirty-one dollars; a fourth, carpenter's tools at six dollars; then smaller sums, here and there.

The Wisconsin man left prison sick, and must have been a public charge here, while his friends would give him a home, if with them, though unable to pay his fare thither.

The Association had not arranged for furnishing the men with clothing, supposing the State would properly attend to that, as previously, through her warden. But as the winter now approached, the society found itself driven to the necessity of helping in this, too, by the fact that the present warden would furnish the men with only the same outfit as in summer, the under-clothes they might happen to have on at the time, added. And, in making out this summer suit, he would construe the letter of the law in the superlative degree, which says, "A suit of cheap clothing,"—he obtaining the cheapest, the most miserably poor. To illustrate, a man left prison in one of those suits, and, before walking a mile, was obliged to call and borrow sewing implements to repair them. The day after, another left, and had worn the shirt furnished him about one day, when, taking him to a shop for the purpose of trying on a coat, I found that one sleeve of the shirt had wholly parted from the body, and the other about half. Another man had worn his pants less than twelve hours when they needed mending.

I went to the shop-keeper and lectured him for such dealing, to which he replied, "I have to be governed by the price the warden will pay. He will not pay for anything better. If he would, I should furnish a better article, and prefer that to this method."

At almost every turn I was met with this money-making system. Well, this could be endured in warm, balmy weather, though truly annoying to the poor fellows; but in the full rigors of the winter of '70 and '71, it was cruel, to say the least.

Let us take a few specimens of this practice. In nearly the severest weather of that winter, a man came to me from the prison to be sent home, some two hundred miles beyond Bangor, Me. As I looked at him I was perfectly astonished that we had a man among us who would think, for a moment, of sending away a dependent, human being, and sickly, too, in such a plight; a rather thin coat, vest and pants that might last him two or three days; no collar, cravat, mittens, overcoat, or boots, but brogans, and those not mates, one of which so pinched his foot that he was forced to remove it shortly after coming in. His person and clothes were filthy indeed, not having seen water for weeks. I could but exclaim, "What a condition! The law says, 'a suit of cheap clothing suited to the season,' and this is such a suit!"

In addition to all this, as the man asserted, the warden asked him, on passing out, "How long do you think it will be before you will contrive to get back here again?" Was not that cool? He himself robbing the fallen one of his just due, a suit of comfortable clothing fitted to the season, and turning him away under those circumstances which would almost of necessity force him to steal to avoid perishing, and then taunt him with such a question?

As yet, our Association had not practiced clothing the men, and of course the warden had no reason to suppose we should.

Keeping my feelings under calm subjection, I went to the prison and asked him if he did not purpose to furnish the man with boots, overcoat, &c., to which he responded in his short, pompous way, "No; when I was deputy here, the men were sent out in just what they happened to have on at the time." After talking till evidently of no further avail, I remarked, "I am a native of New Hampshire, and have some regard for the honor of my State, and I will never disgrace it by sending a man to Maine in such a plight as you propose. I shall fix him up." To which he answered, "I would not carry the matter too far." Well, I did not carry the matter too far, but took the man to the store, shivering by the way, and purchased for him the needed articles, cheap but good,—boots $5.00, overcoat $6.50, and so on,—and returned home with him, where he cast off his "filthy rags," took a warm bath, donned his new under-clothes and came out feeling like a different man, though feeble. He took a bad cold that day by being out in his thin apparel, and passed a hard night, leading us to fear that he would have a fever. But his anxiety helped him the next morning, when he set off, the railroad men giving him a free pass, thus showing that humanity was not all dead in this region.

Soon another was released in a somewhat worse condition, as to clothing, than the above, though with better health. His drawers had one leg wholly minus, the other coming down nearly to the knee, what pretended to remain being in tatters.

Two from western Maine were pardoned one evening and went away early the next morning in the suit given by the warden, without my knowledge. The severe weather must have caused them no little suffering, especially as they must end their journey by a long walk through a deep snow, with their brogans, and one of them was a sickly man.

Another, liberated without my knowledge, started on foot for Providence, R. I., to follow the railroad track. Learning the fact in a few moments, I hastened after him, but to no avail. I heard that his outfit was similar to those above described. I should have clothed him comfortably and furnished a pass by rail, had I overtaken him.

The warden now maintained that he had no concern with the men after leaving prison, and usually took no pains to inform me of their departure; hence, if I did not keep a close watch myself, more or less would leave without my knowledge. My practice usually was to obtain a list each month, from the deputy, of those who would leave during the four following weeks.

The reader will see that I had a good opportunity of knowing the state of the men's under-clothing, from those thus leaving; and further, I would find more or less mending their clothes on the Sabbath. One day a man was at work on his pants, which had become perfectly indecent to wear. On a week day, finding a man in bed in his cell, I inquired if he was sick, to which he replied, "No, I am having my pants mended." Another man brought out the shoes he had been accustomed to wear in prison. No, he could not do that; but they came out; how, I never knew, and he brought them to me. It would be difficult to tell which most abounded, holes or leather. I knew they were his, for I had often seen them on his feet in the prison; though they appeared much worse on a near inspection than at a distance.

An aged prisoner, whose feet were large and lame, wore his shoes sandal fashion, tying them on with such strings as he could find. When I would ask him how he did, he usually replied, "Oh, lame and suffering terribly with my feet." Having nothing but his stockings to protect them from the cold, this must have been severe in winter, though, when in the shop, his fellow prisoners would heat bits of plank and pass to him, on which he could stand and thus be relieved in a measure. I asked him if he could not wear his shoes in the usual way, to which he said, "No, they are too small. Had I very large ones I could. I have asked for such, but they will not obtain me any." The requisite shoes must have been made purposely for the convict, large and of very soft leather, costing, no doubt, more than ordinary shoes. But they would have brought great relief to an old, suffering man.

But our Prison Aid Association, notwithstanding its efforts for good, met those who opposed it. Hence, one told me that the concern was organized for the purpose of running an opposition to the prison, all I could say to which was, "If helping the men, as above described, be running an opposition to the prison, it was organized for that very purpose; otherwise, not." But the man was, no doubt, nettled that the prisoners were looked after on leaving prison, and not permitted to go as the warden provided.

Some, again, pretended that the influence of the Association was in favor of having the prisoners remain in and about Concord. This was the very thing we labored against, or one of them, at least. The Agent, and every active member, invariably used their influence in favor of their going to other places, and especially to keep them away from their old haunts and associations. I knew, however, that there were influences used here, and among prison officers, too, to keep men in the city. Some, for whom I had provided good places away, were tampered with and thus influenced to remain.

23. *Lecturing for the Prison Aid Association.* To widen the influence of this body and become personally acquainted with places where we could send our men for suitable employment and care, the idea was conceived of giving occasional lectures, in favorable localities within the State, on the interests in question. For this purpose, I went out four times during the winter. Besides treating upon the objects and needs of the Association, I alluded to some of the prison matters, such as the proposition in the governor's then late message for the management of the institution to be put under a permanent Board, the responsibility of which the legislature largely shirked, by turning the whole matter into the hands of the governor and council;—for reasons given, the very place where it should not be;— expressed the hope that the next legislature would do its full duty upon the matter; referred also to the much needed repairs just made, and hoped they would be carried still further, improving the manner of lighting the prison by having a small gas jet at each cell, also provide a library room, &c.; but

of course I wholly avoided alluding to the internal management of matters at the institution. My attention was called particularly to this point, however, in one place, by the question being publicly asked by a gentleman, "How are the prisoners treated there?" in reference to which I begged the gentleman to excuse me from answering his question, as I wished to keep the mind on other points. That was true, but it was not the whole of the truth. The question itself was not a proper one to answer then in that place. Could I have conscientiously said, "Well," it would have been done in a moment and been all right, but that I could not do, and besides, I hoped that our rulers would soon get their eyes opened, or the next legislature put things on a proper basis and matters pass off without having anything publicly said. Indeed, I knew but little then of the prison workings in comparison with what I afterwards learned.

---

24. *Prison correspondence under the new rule.* The former warden had solicited me to assist in the correspondence, and I would write for a prisoner occasionally, but pass it to the warden for his examination, till he said, "You need not pass them to me, send them yourself. You know what to write just as well as I do." Hence, I sent a very few in the course of a year without his examination. The reader will understand that all letters, to and from a prisoner, must be thoroughly examined, that nothing prohibited may pass. They are allowed to speak of personal family matters, but nothing of general, secular affairs. The prisoner would not be permitted, of course, to express any dissatisfaction at prison fare or treatment.

The new warden put the entire matter of correspondence into the hands of his deputy, without asking me to do anything about it. Hence, when subsequently solicited to pass a letter as before, I would answer, "I have no right to do that, and can not. You must pass your letter to the deputy." On one occasion, being rather hard pressed to step over the bounds and pass a line, with the assurance it should never be known, &c., &c., I gave the decided negative, adding, "It makes no difference whether known or unknown, the step will be violating the prison rule and my purpose is so to proceed that at all times and under all circumstances, I can say with a clear conscience, I have duly observed every rule." This ended all attempts to influence me in that direction.

Still, I supposed it proper and nothing inconsistent with good prison order, for me to speak of a prisoner's health and success to a friend whom I met outside and to the prisoner of having met the friend and of personal family concerns; or to encourage the prisoners to write to their friends, if thus requested by letter; or to write to friends myself, by request of the prisoners. I did something in this line a very few times, perhaps not a half dozen in all.

Meeting a sister of a prisoner out of the city, one day, I answered her earnest inquiries about his health, and his reform efforts, carrying back to him also a word about her health and a request that he write and send to the new place to which she was about to locate.

A man had a petition before the governor and council for pardon. As agent for our Association, I inquired of him if he had friends to whom he could go, if successful, or what arrangement he would need made for him. He answered that he left friends in England, years before, knew not whether then living or dead, but he would like to return to them if living. Writing as he directed, I soon received a reply stating that some were living, and some were gone, and the earnest desire that he return home at once to see his father alive, of which I informed him, and on account of which his pardon was soon granted, and he left.

Finding a man, who had been here a number of months, in a gloomy and despairing state because friends had not written him since being here, thus giving him reason to feel that they had cast him off, in which case he could not think of living, I wrote to these friends, urging them to what they ought to have performed before. Soon he addressed me, when passing, with a tone of cheer unknown in him since entering prison: "Chaplain, my folks have not cast me off. I have received a good letter from them. They will stand by me, which makes me feel a thousand dollars better." Nor has he learned how his friends were stirred to write.

Thus, in a few cases, I acted in this direction and that for the purpose of removing anxiety without and securing cheer and quietness within, though making no allusions to the one about prison managing or to the other of secular affairs.

---

24 1-2. *Chaplain under a system of espionage.* The former warden had been accustomed to keep his eyes upon the officers, as well as upon the men, to know that everything was moving orderly. The new incumbent took the same course, the correct one so far as that was concerned, in order to keep all matters in the prison perfectly straight. Nor did it lay me under any restraint, as I wished to do right, for the place, in everything, even though no eye might be upon me. My only anxiety in the course would be that I might so walk as to have my steps appear as they really were. Hence, my conduct there was constantly as though under the strictest inspection. And, of course, under these circumstances, I would do nothing but what I supposed to be correct, even if otherwise inclined.

Thus, having passed a number of months with our new warden, a prisoner said, one day, as I approached his cell, "Be careful, Chaplain; they are watching you to see if they can't find some cause for turning you out." Asking no questions, I passed on, not knowing what he meant. But it started a new idea. "Am I under a system of especial surveillance?" I then recollected having seen the guards frequently about where I would be hearing lessons, though I had not noticed but that they were looking after the men. By giving attention now, however, it was plain to see that they were listening to what I said.

At length an overseer left the prison, and, on leaving, unfolded to me the whole matter,—that they were set by the warden to watch my actions, note with whom I conversed, hear what was said, put it down, and report to him. He said, "I was set evenings to watch you from the guard-room, through the spy-hole, but never found anything to report."

Learning this, I could but exclaim, "Consistency indeed! The warden can furnish men enough for a system of espionage over me in the hall, when toiling under such disadvantages and fatigues to help the convicts in their efforts for knowledge, but will not spare even one to guard in the chapel, where I could teach with comparative freedom from all these drawbacks."

Usually, in this cell instruction, we spoke very low, just to hear each other and thus not disturb those in near cells, or interfere with the rule about stillness in the apartment; but, after this discovery, when seeing the guards hanging about, I would purposely speak loud enough for them to hear, and also when the warden himself would be listening to my Sabbath school instruction. And they had the privilege of hearing as good, wholesome truths as I was capable of bringing out.

---

25. *The chaplain's pacific efforts severely taxed.* We are beings of want, and if locked in a cell unable to provide for ourselves, it is wonderful to think how many things we should need to have furnished by others, or suffer. True, we can curtail our wants to a number very much fewer than artificial life would claim, but, when coming to the indispensables, they are not a few. Hence, prisoners, under the kindest treatment and well-furnished with food, clothing, warmth, and all that nature would seem to crave, will need to call more or less frequently for attentions, or find themselves lacking not a little. But under the saving system of this year, calls from the cells must multiply, and, if unheeded, give occasion for uneasiness, angry feelings and disorder. Hence, under such circumstances, the chaplain would naturally be called into the most active service. For, if we can not offer a man food enough to satisfy the cravings of his appetite, the next thing is to reconcile his mind to going without, or so engross his thoughts, that he shall not so

keenly feel the gnawings of hunger. Or, if one is cold, and we can not bring the means of warmth, by presenting a satisfactory excuse or interesting the intellect, we may do him essential service in helping him calmly endure what he otherwise could not.

Precisely on these principles I acted, and engrossed the prisoner's attention as earnestly and interestingly as possible, always, when practicable, taking special pains to immediately furnish the thing called for; or to excuse, when I could; or turn one's sufferings to as profitable a lesson as could be, to him. Hence, when the cold was reigning almost unmitigated in the cells, for a few days, I would repeat to one and another what I heard the warden say, that "the water was low and he feared it would wholly fail." Among the replies, one said, "Well, then, we must bear it the best we can, though it is hard."

One day, coming to a man's cell to hear a lesson, he said, "I have no lesson, I have been in the solitary. They did so and so to me, at which I got mad, and would not do as they wished, and they put me in there." I thought it likely, from the circumstances, that the impatience of an officer and his irritating course had much, too much, to do with the matter. But that was not for me to hint at, even. I rather said, "Well, you say you got mad and have been in the solitary. See what you have suffered for getting mad. How much better for you to govern your temper. You know where you are, what you did to bring yourself here. You understand what is required, and that refusal on your part is of no avail. Now, why not govern yourself, no matter what they say? If you really think they bear hard upon you, control your angry passions, and do what they require as cheerfully and promptly as possible. Thus, you can become accustomed here to governing yourself, that, when you go out, you will be the better able to meet the vexations of the world. Now, will you not try this course?" He replied, "I don't know, Chaplain, it is a hard case." In a few days he remarked, "Chaplain; I have been almost constantly thinking of what you said the other day, have come to the conclusion that your way is the best, and am resolved to attempt putting it in practice." With most hearty congratulations on his new resolve, I left him again. Some weeks after I received from his lips this satisfactory report: "Well, Chaplain, I have been practicing your method since our last conversation, and find it works like a charm. I have but little trouble now, and am determined to keep on as I have begun." Thus he proceeded till released. This man was naturally irritable and easily angered. He had not previously labored to control himself in regard to this important point; but now, when summoning all his better powers to the task, he resolutely addressed his mind to it, and a noble victory was his.

There was another man here who also could be easily aroused, but was perhaps still more stubborn, when angry. He, too, had been an inmate of the solitary more or less. To him I appealed in a manner similar to the above, and, after persistent labors, succeeded in inducing him to earnestly try the proposed course, and with like results. But he was a man who needed frequent encouragement to help him calmly endure the vexations and annoyances almost constantly surrounding him. Hence, he maintained his self-control and kept from trouble while he had one to labor for his continuance in well-doing, but afterwards he fell into difficulty again, and would consequently become an inmate of the solitary. Thus I proceeded, and, by assiduous efforts, robbed this dark abode of many hours of occupancy.

There were others not rendering themselves liable to the dungeon, but who would become filled with angry, revengeful emotions at what they were forced to endure. I would labor to induce these to use what they experienced as a means of self-culture, to leave the acts of others in the hands of God, submit calmly to what they could not avoid, do their own duties faithfully, and in all things keep themselves strictly in the right. Thus I was almost constantly called to speak a word here and a word there to a pacific end, and labored untiringly in that direction.

In the women's department, also, these efforts were found needed. One of the inmates, whom we will call K., had often caused them no little trouble. With all their efforts, she would contrive to keep almost a constant broil among them. Hence, I decided to see what could be done, in her case, by moral and religious efforts. Therefore, one Sabbath, after our usual service, I remained awhile for personal conversation with the inmates respecting their desires and feelings on the subject of reform, purposely coming to K. last. After conversing awhile with her on religious subjects, I came to the direct inquiry, "Now, K., will you not turn from your former course and seek to become a true Christian?" She looked upon me as though perfectly astonished at the question, and answered, "Why, Chaplain, that would be of no sort of use. Here I have been going on in my career of life these twenty years, and, should I attempt to turn now and become good, no one would put the least confidence in me. It is of no kind of use." I labored to assure her that she was mistaken in this idea, that would she truly repent and turn from evil, people would see it, and learn to confide in her the same as in others who had reformed, also asserting that she had the power for making of herself a most excellent, useful woman, if she would use it aright. I referred to what she might have been, what she had lost, how much she had suffered, the condition to which she had brought herself, and the prospect still before her, if she went on. At length the tears began to glisten in her eyes; she yielded and said, "Chaplain, I will try." The next Sabbath I asked her how she succeeded, with the answer, "Not much, but I am trying the best I can." Retiring from their room, I asked the attendant how they had prospered the past week. "Oh," said she, "first rate. We have had a perfect reformation. Everything has been peaceful and quiet, no fretting and scolding,—a perfect change." And so it was when I left the prison. But I learned that K., after my leaving, became discouraged, was thrown from the track and returned to her former habits. And no wonder, there was so great a lack of prudence and skill in managing there, so much of a vexatious character.

My position was one of difficulty, needing all the wisdom and discretion I could command. The prisoners were looking to me for direction on the one hand, while jealous watchfulness followed every step on the other.

Thus I went on, constantly doing what I could for the best good of the institution in whatever way practicable. No matter what course others took concerning me or the prison, my duty was to act with fidelity and in the fear of God, which I endeavored sacredly to do.

One rule I constantly carried with me, never deviating from it on any occasion, which rule was, not to give a word, or hint even, against any prison officer or prison move. This seemed essential to the best being of the prisoner. For, if really wronged, my deviation from that rule would tend to impress him more deeply, make him feel his wrong more keenly, and excite to greater irritability, resulting, on his part, perhaps, in more disorderly acts, and, consequently, greater trouble. Then, on my own part, such a deviation must be perfect suicide, so far as the plan might be concerned, showing the authorities conclusively that I was unfit for the position, and giving them the most urgent reasons for putting another in my place.

A moderate share of common sense would teach one to keep very wide of such deviation. Then it could be of no avail. If censurable things were being done in the prison management, the rulers were the parties for one to approach respecting them, those having the power to apply the remedy.

———

26. *Death of Gideon Sylver.* This man had been in the army, was a good soldier, strong and vigorous; very quiet and obedient; faithful to his task and never complaining, but seemed intent on doing the best he could to please those over him and thus share their good will. He was set to carrying lumber in and out of the dry room, exposed to extremes of heat and cold, at times perhaps having wet feet from want of proper shoes, till, failing in health, complaining of distress about the chest, the doctor ordered him to lighter and less exposed work, when he was set to running a planer, said, however, to be a very hard machine to run, though subsequently made easier by rollers attached. Here he grew no better, but had severe attacks.

One day, in his distress, he fell on his knees, girding his arms about him and groaning repeatedly. The deputy took him from the shop and returned him relieved. But soon he wholly failed, was taken away for the last time and kept in his cell, part of the time quiet and then groaning more or less intensely. To my inquiry about the locality of his distress, he put his hand over the left lung. Sabbath evening, Feb. 10th, I think, his distress came on with great severity, he, making no little ado, said, to my inquiry whether he needed anything more, "I have a powder to take, which will no doubt relieve me," and appeared disposed to make the best of his condition. Meeting the steward, I asked if all was being done for the man that could be, with the answer, "Yes, I think there is. The fact is, not much ails him. He is nervous; thinks he is dreadful sick, and makes a great ado." I passed on, thinking that Sylver must be a very sick man notwithstanding these views, that, when one naturally so patient and quiet makes such demonstrations, there must be reason for immediate assistance. It seemed to me that the hospital was the proper place for him, and that he ought to be there receiving suitable warmth and close attention. But understanding that I might say no more, and meddle no farther, I retired, feeling that the man was in a forlorn condition.

The cold in the hall was not as severe now as formerly, for the weather had become milder without, and that coal stove, before referred to, stood not far from Sylver's cell. This helped in a measure, but came short of the warmth needful to a sick man like him. Things passed thus, with more or less of his moaning when I was in, till Wednesday evening, on which, by reason of the prayer meeting, I did not visit the apartment. Thursday noon I heard no moaning, but when the men had retired for their work, I called to visit the sufferer and found his cell empty, he having been carried to the hospital. I went to my dinner, purposing to return and visit the hospital immediately after; but, being detained, at length saw a coffin carried to the prison, and, on inquiry, learned that Sylver was dead. He died a few minutes past twelve, when I was known to be at work in the hall, but nothing was said to me about the event. How my heart sank within me, though, of the events of that terrible Wednesday night, I then knew nothing. The facts subsequently came to light in their revolting features. They were gathered from the steward, overseers, guard and released prisoners, investigated with all care, and are, no doubt, correct, as follows:

Sylver grew worse Wednesday evening, groaning often. The steward came, and, after giving him the usual attention, said, "Now, Sylver, there is no use in your making such a fuss as this. Dry up and go to sleep." Sylver replied, "I would, if I could; but my sufferings are so great I can't help it;" to which the steward responded, "Yes, you can, if you only think so. Dry up, if you don't want to go into the solitary," and left, with the groans falling on his ears as he passed from the apartment.

At nine the night watch went to his task in the hall, and found the inmate almost incessantly groaning, with interludes of prayer,—"Lord have mercy on me; do help me; forgive my sins," and so on, also suffering intensely with the cold, locked in his cell that none could approach him in attempts at relief. The watchman's heart was stirred, for humanity's promptings were not dead in him. He looked about for something that might afford warmth to the agonized man, and found some bricks, which he warmed and passed through the grating to the sufferer, who for a time had strength to take and place them around him for relief.

The other prisoners could not sleep. Raps would be heard from one and another for the watch to go to them and explain. Others would cry out, "Call the deputy and have that man cared for." At about eleven, the prisoners began to stir determinedly, when the watch called a guard and sent for the deputy to come and care for Sylver. But he gave no heed to the summons, except to send the guard back to the hall, who went to the sick man's cell, made efforts to still him, and left. Those near said they heard the word *gag* there used, and understood that the sufferer was receiving threats of being gagged, in case he did not stop his noise.

As the guard retired from the hall, all hope of relief for the doomed one came fully to an end, he being now literally left to his fate. He would still engage in prayer,—"Lord, have mercy on my soul; Lord, why won't they come and do something for my relief?"

Had the cell door been left unlocked, the watch could have done much more towards affording the needed warmth, and been more effective in efforts for his relief. But that privilege would not be allowed. At length the man became too weak and exhausted to take and use the proffered bricks, which ended the offices of kindness the watch was struggling to perform. Finally, the moaning grew more and more faint, and was of such a tone as to give clear indication that death had commenced its work. The sad hours wore slowly away. The morning finally arrived, and the men were called to their tasks, the now feeble moans dying upon their ears as they passed out. At length, when suiting his convenience, the warden went to the dying man's cell. Seeing the result of their work, he hastened for the doctor, whom he found just starting on an imperative call. But he hurried to the prison to see the man a moment and direct the means to be used till his return. He found him thoroughly cold, as though dead, and ordered him to be taken at once to the hospital, the most vigorous rubbing to be used by two men, and other means for restoring warmth. For a time he revived somewhat, but these efforts, however beneficial they might have been in season, were of no avail now, for death soon closed the scene.

The brothers, summoned by a telegram, were present in a few hours. A post-mortem examination was had, at which one asked, "What was the matter with the man?" to which the doctor answered, "Probably some difficulty about the heart." An invited physician responded,—"From what I hear, I think it a clear case of congestion of the lungs;" one of the worst cases of which, it was found to be. A consulting physician said that the case must have been a number of days in progress.

The reader must make his own comment on this whole affair.[2] My feelings were never more stirred. We were terribly shocked at Pike's murder of the Browns, those feeble, old people. But he dispatched them at once; neither, perhaps, experiencing a moment's sensibility of suffering. True, the man lived a number of hours, but was probably not sensible of pain. But Sylver, in his agonies, begging and pleading for help, was forced to pass that terrible night carefully locked in his cell, and no heed given to his cries. Had they ended his sufferings with a single blow, without any threats of the dungeon or gag, he would have been thereby saved from the piercing agonies of those slowly dragging hours. Would not that have been compassion in comparison with what they did? But one says, "That would have been murder." True, and what was that treatment in reality? With due care and attention the man might have recovered, but they so proceeded that it was absolutely impossible for him to live. No man with a lung difficulty could survive such treatment. The blow of an ax, severing his head from his body, could have been no surer means of death.

[2] Important facts on this matter are withheld in the narrative above, as the possessors were unwilling, at the examination, to divulge them publicly except under the shield of an oath.

I know the deputy attempted to exonerate himself from blame before the governor and council, by asserting that the guard, sent for him, failed to do his errand correctly, and that he understood himself called to still the noise among the men, and for this sent the guard back.

Had that really been the case, why did not the guard go among the men and endeavor to still them? Why go to Sylver's cell and expend his efforts there? Or, admitting the deputy's statement to be true, did that help the matter for him in the least? If summoned by the watch to quell a rising tumult, was he, as an officer, acting the part of duty by remaining quietly in bed and sending nothing but a guard to the work, who could effect no more than the watch himself? All the circumstances combined in forcing one, understanding the matter, to the conclusion that they acted knowingly and intentionally respecting the man.

Do not understand me as charging them with intentionally and deliberately murdering their victim, for this I do not, but that he fell a sacrifice to a system of prison management that they were intent on establishing; a system under which the officers are to be the sole judges of the prisoners' needs, use them as they may choose, put them in whatever condition they may see fit, and they in turn not allowed to utter a word, nor give the slightest expression of feeling any more than the dumb, driven ox. If they die, "it is of no account; he is only a prisoner," as an officer said to me, respecting another who had died.

On entering the hall the evening after Sylver's cruel death, I found the prisoners greatly excited. One exclaimed, as loud as he thought prudent, "Murder! murder! They have murdered one of our number." Another remarked, "Well, we see what the fate of any of us may be, if taken sick." Marked anxiety was depicted upon all their countenances; and who would wonder?

---

27. *The Sylver case excitement and hearing before the Governor and Council.* The brothers were greatly aroused at what they could see and gather about this death, felt that deep iniquity had been practiced in connection with it, and resolved on a criminal prosecution of the warden. But, finding, from legal counsel, that they probably could not make a case in that line hold, they were thrown into doubt respecting what to attempt.

Meanwhile the story of the affair spread in the community, carrying with it exaggerated reports, that "Sylver was really murdered; was gagged and left to die alone," and thus on. When passing the streets in the city, I would be inquired of, if such were really the facts, to which I would respond in the negative, that he died in the hospital with attendants about him, but could explain no farther. Execrations at the prison management were often heard.

Whether true or not, I never ascertained, but report had it, that the doctor felt called upon to demand an investigation of the affair before the governor and council, and that the warden favored looking into the other departments, and so a hearing was appointed to be had at the council chamber one Friday evening, in the latter part of February, or in early March. I was summoned to be present, but with no intimation for what purpose. The Sylvers, when cherishing the idea of a criminal prosecution, had looked about a little for evidence, and had secured the statements of an overseer at the prison, when the death occurred, written out in the form of an affidavit and sworn to before a justice of the peace, and also those of a released prisoner. These were in the hands of the lawyer they had employed, or purposed to employ, to manage for them. This lawyer appeared, but it was understood that the brothers had become disheartened and ceased to interest themselves in looking up evidence, preparing for a thorough investigation of the death in question; why, we know not. None were put on oath, hence the hearing failed of bringing out important matter, as the men having it, would not divulge unless under oath.

I was called on first to testify and asked to state about the Sylver case, but, as before related, I then knew but little of material value. The transactions of that Wednesday night, I had, at that time, heard something of, but to me they were only matters of report, and among the points requiring the efficacy of the oath to bring them out. Hence, I could say nothing of them. I was asked some questions about the prison living, but on points concerning which I knew but little, and then was turned directly to my own prison management. It seemed by the questioning that, in this summary manner, with no opportunity to prepare for defense, I was virtually put on trial for a violation of prison rules on two points,—the correspondence, and passing information to prisoners,—and called on to testify against myself. But I had nothing to cover up, had acted in all cases as I thought to be right, so frankly stated my whole proceedings in the matters, as near as I could recollect on the spur of the moment, and also explained my motives, excepting that I could not, of course, allude to anything of the warden's procedure as making my efforts especially needful to the best order of the prison. No one else was called to testify on these points; but I was kept standing during the narrations and questionings till so far exhausted that, perhaps between ten and eleven, I had to ask the privilege of sitting.

Then I was called on to state about my lecturing for the Prison Aid Association, whether I had alluded to the prison or not. Having become somewhat confused in mind, for the time, I could not recollect a single allusion I had made, and therefore answered unqualifiedly, "I have not," not thinking to say, "I have not to my present recollection." The Governor replied, "There must be some mistake in the matter, for I have received two letters from places where those lectures were given, stating differently," and he called for another witness.

As to the Sylver matter, the effort was made to leave the impression on the mind that the patient really died of a heart difficulty, though he probably would have died of the congestion, but not so soon. No pretense, however, was made that any unhealthy condition was found about the heart, except in the attending physician's assertion, that, on puncturing the pericardium; a little gas, as he thought, whizzed out, and that he recollected of having read in two medical works, of cases where such a gas collection had proved fatal. The physicians whom the Sylvers employed on the post mortem, were not present, and hence no light was gained from that source.

The lawyer presented the written statements of the released prisoner, referring to the death, the cold, food matters, &c., at the prison, but this was summarily swept from the board by the testimony of the steward: "There is not a word of truth in his statement." I happened to know personally, then, that some of the points in that statement were true, and what I did not know myself agreed exactly with the general testimony of the men leaving prison. But I was not referred to on the point and thus that testimony was useless. The affidavit from the overseer, I think, was not presented.

At about two o'clock at night, the hearing was adjourned until the next Monday evening, after which I arranged with the Governor to see him Monday, P. M. I saw the letters referred to, which contained the grossest misrepresentations, uttering sentiments I never thought of, or, if I had, should not have expressed there, unless demented.

I went home with a strong conviction that efforts were being made, by whom I knew not, to turn the whole force of thought upon me and make of me a scape goat in the matter. I retired, but not to shut my eyes in sleep for the night. For a time my mind remained in confusion about those lectures, but after resting awhile, and the excitement had passed off, all came clearly to view, as given on a former page.

28. *Preparing for the adjourned session.* Saturday morning I wrote to a few understanding and reliable gentlemen, who heard the lectures in question, alluded to the letters and their allegations, and by return mail received answers, asserting that, as nearly as they understood, and by inquiry from others who heard, no such ideas were received as charged in the missives, giving some ideas that were uttered, a very different sentiment from the letters, and what no one could censure. That day, I met the writer of one of those letters in the city, and to my inquiry, he replied, "Oh, I did not hear the lecture, or know anything about what was said, personally; but my son was present, and gave me what information I had." I could but think, "A bright son that!"

In the afternoon, I called on the Governor as appointed, and found him very much excited over the matter. He talked almost incessantly for a long time, but occasionally giving me opportunity for putting in a word. I attempted to assure him that he was laboring under a great mistake about my acts at the prison, that I had not been guilty of anything he had in mind, and that he must have been misinformed. But my assurances seemed to carry but little weight. He finally said, "Mr. Quinby, your management at the prison has caused me more trouble and anxiety than all my State business put together." I was perfectly astonished. There were my incessant and most arduous labors for peace and quietness in the institution, my great painstaking, with the sole view of leading the prisoners to do right in every respect, with never a hint from me, to a prisoner, of disapprobation of any prison officer or his acts,—with never a word of dispute between any of us as officers, besides my careful observance of all the prison rules to the letter, as I understood them, to which I had ever felt impelled by a sense of duty, and on which, for a long while, I had felt the importance of double and thribble care. How could my management in these things cause the Governor such trouble and anxiety? The truth now flashed in mind, that setting the guards and overseers to watch me, had its purpose. Then, there must have been a long and persistent course of running to his Excellency with a tissue of misrepresentations. Had it really befallen me as it befel the man going down from Jerusalem to Jericho? Things certainly looked in that direction, and perhaps it was nothing more than might have been anticipated; for, if one would persistently slander innocent ladies, it would be natural for him to misrepresent me. If, at every opportunity, he would defame the character of another, could I rationally suppose that mine would be any safer in his hands?

Having left the Governor with the settled conviction that my days of incessant prison toil were virtually ended, a gentleman of influence in the place, rode up to me in haste, with the remark, "Step aboard, Mr. Quinby, you must have legal counsel in these matters. A combination is formed to crush you, and the really guilty go free. I have volunteered to engage such lawyers, and they wish to see you at once to learn the true state of things and how to take hold of the case." Though I insisted that it would be of no avail, he gave no heed to that, and soon landed me at the proposed office door. I related, in brief, the general facts as they had occurred, and the interview just had with the Governor, to which the eldest of the number replied, "Your case is a foregone conclusion. It is already decided. You can not do a thing." But another proposed to consult with the attorney already in the work, and arrange as thought advisable.

Returning home, I found a friend waiting to inform me of the proffered service of still another lawyer. Thus friends were aroused and clustered around ready to help, as I had not anticipated. No little excitement prevailed in the place.

29. *The adjourned hearing.* I went to this with ideas clear, thoughts collected, mind pretty thoroughly aroused, and feeling ready to attempt a vindication of the right. Being again called on first, I commenced, referred to the assertion that I made the previous evening about not alluding to the prison in my lectures, that I was wrong in this, that I did refer to it, stating on what

points, and the sentiments uttered, presenting the letters that I had received, showing that I uttered no such ideas as alleged, and gave a general outline of my reform moves at the prison and the motives that impelled me to voluntarily assume such excessive labors, closing thus: "And now, gentlemen, if, after doing all this, I am to be crushed, it will be a hard case."

They now referred to the other cases on which but little more was brought out. Before closing, one of the council, turning to me, remarked, "Now, Mr. Quinby, if you know of anything wrong at the prison, not here developed, we wish you to be free and state it, for we desire to understand the truth." But I did not think it best for me to say anything farther then, for, if I did, it would be opening a square fight with the warden, which I by no means desired, and for which I did not feel myself prepared. It would have been really stepping forward as leader in the matter, a position which I did not wish. Then, again, as I supposed, such prejudice had somehow been aroused against me, that, should I attempt to make further development, it would be of little or no use, and perhaps be worse for the cause than my silence. Besides, I hoped that the time would come, and that not far distant, when our rulers would have their eyes opened, and matters be so effectually sifted as to find the real truth.

Thus, the hearing closed, and we left the deliberating body to make up judgment, which was that "no blame is to be attached to any one," or to that amount. This was just as I had anticipated respecting the Sylver case, the food, &c., for the investigation really amounted to little in those respects. I was truly disappointed, however, concerning myself, not that any wrong, or even a shadow of it, was brought against me, but, as I judged from the Governor's remarks and the general drift of things, that certain ones had worked underhandedly, and so effectually as to render my removal a sure matter. But they did not succeed.

30. *Motives for desiring the chaplain's removal.* One asks, "What could be the motive of any for seeking your removal, if you had uniformly proceeded at the prison as before set forth?" That was the puzzle to me, for not a word had been said in that direction, except the note of warning from the prisoner, till conversing with the Governor, and then nothing specific; hence, I was left wholly to conjecture. My persistent effort to keep alive, as far as possible, what I could of the reform system of the past year, was, no doubt, repulsive to the warden, and in order to be rid of that, he would need to be rid of me. This might be one motive. Again, no little stir was being made in the city about prison usages, prison suffering, &c. Probably he thought I was at the bottom of that; that I wrote down facts inside, and divulged them outside. Hence, the nettling that one of my practices caused.

Occasionally, I would be solving a long question in arithmetic for the prisoner at the striking of the signal for retiring to the shop, at which I would step aside, sit down, finish my solution, return the slate to the prisoner's cell, and leave. I also, at times, noticed that the deputy was watching me far more earnestly than the men. Then the question was asked at the hearing, what I was writing on these occasions.

Now, if he considered me as the cause of this stirring up, he, of course, would wish me away. This would be a strong motive. But I was not. True, I wrote the stories of a number of the men, as they came out, or till all were found telling over and over the very same thing, in substance. These, however, I laid away in my drawer, saying nothing about them to any one. But these men would also call on their former Sabbath school teachers, or other acquaintances they had met in prison, and relate to them their stories, and thus they spread. Neighbors would call at my house, and be talking these matters over, I being as reticent as possible, but would not come out squarely and lie in the matter by contradicting the accounts. And, further, the points which I had brought to the governor's notice were, without doubt, unsatisfactory to the warden. Then, also, my fitting up the prisoners as they left. He perhaps desired a man for the place, who might wish it so much as to be willing to pass on with doing but little of what I was attempting.

For months I supposed these the great motives which prompted that removal. But the next year I learned of another and perhaps greater than either of these. A man, retiring from prison, said to me, "Chaplain, how amused we would feel sometimes, last year, when you were preaching, at the appearance of the warden, to see him turn pale, and then red, and hitch on his seat. We understood it." Another, usually present, not a prisoner, said also that he had noticed the same thing.

At the time in question, I was treating upon the moral code from Sabbath to Sabbath, and would, in one discourse, take up lying, and point out as clearly as I could its influence upon the one practicing it, and upon society in general; then, perhaps, stealing, or swindling and thus on. In these efforts, I was intent on discharging my duty to the prisoners, on leading them from those sins, having nothing to do in the matter with the warden as to any of his steps in life. If personal applications were made, I was not responsible for that. I arranged for no such purpose.

But when the man, on his release, made the remark given, the idea flashed in my mind that here was a stirring motive to efforts for getting rid of me, with the hope of obtaining one who might be willing, on coming to certain sins, to let the plow of truth turn out, and not go straight through.

Whether that running to the Governor and that stirring him up so greatly, was prompted by one or another of the above reasons, or all combined, or something else, still, I never ascertained. Had charges been preferred against me openly and squarely, I could have met them face to face, known what was what, and shown their falsity. But as things were, I was left in the dark as to how to proceed, and to what conclusions I should come as to the motives prompting to the struggle to my disadvantage.

----

31. *Chaplain's change of course and the question as to who should conduct the prison correspondence.* After this hearing, I decided to change my course in two respects, the one about going out to lecture on Association matters, the other about writing to prisoners' friends. These I wholly abandoned. True, nothing was said to me suggestive of these changes, nor had I taken any wrong step on the points, but, in the investigation, I was led to see that these were *the* sources whence misconception would be the most likely to arise, and where evil-minded persons might pretend a wrong, with some show of plausibility, without really any shadow of grounds in truth. I would not only shun every evil, but every appearance of evil, or what might be construed into an appearance.

Great sensitiveness pervades too many minds on the idea of attempting to show benevolence to a released prisoner, they holding it as a wrong to society. These will not hear on the subject understandingly, but with prejudice and a proclivity to misrepresent. Though the class does not embrace, in its numbers, the more intelligent, worthy citizens, yet it contains more or less who possess the power of casting mists of blindness before the well-disposed and honest seekers for the right.

In this class, we find the ideas of the brutal and vindictive freely cropping out in their utterances. "Those fellows ought to suffer. They were put in prison for punishment, now let them have enough of it, so that they may thus learn to do better, no matter if it were ten times worse." These persons seem to think that the correct way of prison management would be to select the most hard-hearted, cruel men of the State for officers, and deliver the convicts into their hands, for them to exercise their brutal feelings upon as fully and freely as they may choose. These points, then, evidently need to be agitated in the State, by lecturers and through the press, but it were better that this work be done by others than by the prison chaplain.

The loss of my occasional writing was severely felt, especially by outside friends. Thus, on Fast day of '71, a prisoner wrote a letter to a sister in the West, and asked for an envelope and stamp that he might send it, but weeks and months passed and none were forthcoming. There was the idea, "You must not ask a second time." The sister became deeply troubled at not hearing from or about the brother, not knowing whether he were dead or alive, and wrote to me, earnestly beseeching to be informed. But as I was now under the ban, I did not answer her. She also wrote to the ex-warden, but he was away and did not answer. In the fall, when that gentleman of Concord was chosen warden, she wrote to him, but, as he was sick and knew nothing of the matter, he did not respond. And no doubt she also wrote to the warden himself; but probably has not heard to this day.

Formerly, I should have written her something like this: "Your brother is alive, in usual health, and progressing well. Don't be over-anxious till he may write you." In this way I could have satisfied her, measurably, at least with no reflection, in any way, on prison management.

This neglect of the deputy seemed the more cruel from the fact that the man was a most faithful, obedient prisoner, and that this sister had previously furnished him with ample writing materials, that he might write frequently with no expense to the State, which materials the warden had confiscated on coming into office.

In connection with this matter, the important question comes up, In whose hands, really, should the prison correspondence be placed?—in those of the warden or chaplain? The correspondence, to be well managed, requires no little labor, especially if the inmates are permitted to write as they should and receive answers in return. If, in the warden's hands, it would tend to crowd other business too much, or itself be too much neglected, the latter having been the fact.

To avoid all this, in various places, they put the management in the hands of the chaplain. This would seem the more appropriate, being rather in his line of duty, and more easily performed by him. A schedule of the points of information, which should be allowed to pass, could be marked out by the competent authority and laid before him for his guidance, that matters might be correct in that respect.

This question ought to receive the careful attention of our law-makers, for proper letter writing should not be restricted in any degree in the prison. Good letters from home and friends will bring with them no little reformatory power and influence to quietness and order. Indeed, the privilege, by proper management, can be made a great force in disciplinary efforts among the prisoners.

---

32. *Change, for a time, in the warden's management.* Shortly after the death of Sylver, a man, occupying a cell near by, was taken sick, but could sit up the most of the time. As he said, the warden went to him and remarked, "I am warden here. Be free, and ask for whatever you need, and you shall have it."

He permitted this man to sit with his cell door unlocked, and to go to the stove when he chose, and, to all appearance, properly cared for him, giving reason for much commendation. True, he was shortly to leave prison, and his statement would go towards counteracting the reports of prison cruelty circulating outside, and some were uncharitable enough to contend that this was the object of the better treatment.

One evening, about this time, I found a prisoner in his cell appearing as though he could live but a few hours, and perhaps minutes, unless immediately attended to. He had been in the hospital a number of weeks with a lung difficulty and, though he had not recovered, was transferred sometime that day, I think, to his cell,—to a colder atmosphere. Here, he found it difficult to speak or breathe. I hastened to the warden for him to attend to the matter. He hurried for the physician, who soon arrived, and had the sufferer returned to the hospital, where he died some weeks after. This was one of my only three requests or suggestions that were granted or favorably attended to by the warden while I was under him. True, I was not denied many times, for I early learned not to propose anything or make any request, except when absolutely needed.

This changed course in the warden, however, did not continue many weeks. That hearing and its acquittal had passed, and the Sylver affair was dying away, when, at length, I thus found him returned to his former spirit. Though early in the season, on a warm day, he had divested the sick of their flannels, and I suppose all other prisoners. Soon the weather became cooler, and I found a sick man in the hospital suffering greatly for want of his flannels, which articles, as he asserted, he had not previously been without, summer or winter, for twenty years. He was trembling with the cold, which much enhanced his distress. Going to the warden, I presented the case, and received the reply, "If he wants his flannels, let him ask the doctor." He could meddle in the matter enough to divest the man of the needed articles, but would not move to put them on, and thus mitigate his sufferings. It was then early in the afternoon, and the man would have to suffer till the next forenoon, the usual time for the doctor to make his visit. When he came, as I was informed, he lectured them severely for removing the flannels at all.

---

33. *The fate of Henry Stewart and others.* Henry was said to have been exceedingly unfortunate in his parents, they having been largely chargeable with his proclivities to evil. He was highly excitable, easily thrown into a perfect phrensy of passion, insane at times, and, on the whole, very difficult to manage, requiring a large amount of patience and skill in those over him. They needed to study his peculiarities and accommodate their treatment to

his particular case, much the same as would the driver of a vicious, balky horse. The former managers had so treated him, that he had really improved, and his condition was appearing more and more hopeful. But in the new order, where officers were not expected to bother themselves over peculiarities, it was different with Henry. Though laboring with faithfulness generally, what was bred within would appear in outward acts. When a spell came on, they would "shake him up," as the deputy said (the import of which I did not fully understand), and put him in the solitary. At length his insanity, or whatever had impelled him, would pass off, and he come out in his right mind. Confinement to his cell would probably have been just as effective in securing his good deportment and less injurious to his health. Whenever I visited him, he would appear hopeful, tell what a good boy he proposed to be, how he meant to live, and not get into any more trouble; that he should soon be out, and would then strive to be a good man. Many air castles the poor fellow thus built, but to see them fall. The prison fare and general management was now highly unfavorable to his proclivities, tending constantly to make them worse. Men repeatedly told me that the officers would severely beat him, and that he was sadly abused. One day, in a freak of insanity or anger, he struck his overseer to the floor with a bed-post, coming within a hair's breadth of ending his life, and was aiming a second blow, which a fellow prisoner arrested, and thus saved the overseer. Henry was put in the solitary, and I know not how long kept there, nor how used; but when, at length, I found him in his cell, he was greatly changed. I was perfectly astonished! He was not only insane, but changed in physical appearance; shrunken in flesh and with a strange expression of countenance. For a time, I could hardly believe it was Henry, but finally had to admit that it was really he. I have seldom seen one with a fever change more for the time. Soon his insanity took a boisterous turn by night, keeping the other prisoners all awake, which induced them for a time to confine him to the solitary during these hours, and keep him in his cell by day. But his howls so disturbed the prison family, that they next resorted to keeping him in the shop by night, lying upon his back, his feet chained together, with a post between them.

Thus, they continued for a season, but finally, the governor sent him to the insane asylum. Shortly after, I was speaking to one of Henry, in hearing of the warden, as being insane, to which he replied, "No, he is not insane. He is ugly, of which I could have cured him, had his time not been so near out." I thought, "You *would* have cured him by death, and were very near it."

As he was taken to the asylum, the warden said to me, "Chaplain, I wish it understood that he is taken out to be tried for attempting to kill his overseer," thereby expressing the desire, as I understood it, for me to give that version of the matter to the prisoners. "What an idea!" I answered in my mind, "the chaplain going about lying for the warden!"

Fisher was naturally of a low order of mind, but still possessed knowledge enough to work well at many things under the direction of another, was to come out the early part of March, but whom I missed from his cell a while previous, and, from his long absence, began to suppose they had sent him off unbeknown to me. But the day previous to the expiration of his sentence, I found him again in his cell, completely demented. I was told by more than one, that his overseer, attempting to direct him in a certain way about his work and not succeeding, seized him by the collar, plunged him head foremost to the floor, and then jerked him about, he probably now uttering some disrespectful words; then the deputy was called and took him to the solitary, I was also informed, and plunged him against the outer prison door, on the way, with such force as to push it open.

When first finding him in his cell, as stated, I asked where his father lived, and he answered, "Enfield," as I understood it. But after that, I could not obtain even a sound from his lips. He kept almost constantly spitting, would frequently laugh to himself, but I could learn nothing about his legal residence. I was expected to care for him, and would not turn him loose to suffer and perhaps perish; but I found that I should be liable for damage, should I send him to another town. True, the State, by her prison management, had reduced him to this wretched condition, and ought to bear the expense of maintaining him, but there was no law or provision for that. Hence, finding it my only safe and legitimate course, I obtained a decree from the probate judge, took him to the insane asylum, and notified the commissioners of that county, of the same.

No doubt, with proper prison fare and treatment, both of these men might have come out able to earn their living, under proper guardians, which they would have needed; and that the fate of both was directly chargeable to the prison treatment.

There was one, also, who left after my departure from prison, belonging to another State, who had become nearly as demented as Fisher. Hence, they obtained for him a railroad pass, and put him on board the cars with a label fastened upon his arm, directing him to be transferred to such a State and town, where his friends were supposed to live. He, too, I doubt not, was reduced to that demented condition by the prison treatment for he was far from such a state at the beginning of the year.

---

34. *Warden's want of courtesy to prisoners' visitors.* By rule, no friend is allowed to see a prisoner except in presence of the warden or a subordinate that he

may hear whatever is said. The time allowed for a visit is usually short, and the parties, of course, wish to make the most of every moment. But no little complaint was made, that, when the interview was in the warden's presence, he would engross much of the time in recounting his exploits in prison management, the disorders he found, the corrections he had made, how they would deceive his predecessor, but could not deceive him, and the like. No matter how far one had come, or at what expense, he would, perhaps, be treated thus. Some, on going away, having had an opportunity of saying but few words to the prisoner whom they visited, would utter remarks which were anything but complimentary to the man thus imposing upon them, as they regarded it, and to the State for allowing such things to occur.

---

35. *Effects of the new order upon the prisoners.* The mental effects have been spoken of in three cases. These were the most marked of that type. The effects on the physical system were also very apparent. It could not be otherwise, for the men lost no little flesh. One man said he weighed himself about the time the order in question commenced, and found his weight some one hundred and eighty pounds. He left after being under the system a little more than six months, and had lost some twenty-five pounds in weight. And I should judge this to be a fair general average, according to their appearance, of the change in most of the prisoners.[3]

[3] The Bill of Fare at the prison for this year can not be given, as it was not, to the writer's knowledge, published.

And why not this result? A large number did not pretend to eat any dinner on Mondays, and many more ate but little. There was such a general carrying back of the food at this meal, that I decided to count particularly and see exactly what the facts were. On two consecutive Mondays in April, I think, I did this and found a dozen or over, not even taking their dishes to their cells, so had nothing to eat; thirty-two each day, returned their basins, all, I think, with the bit of bread gone, a large number not having touched the wheat part, some having eaten a very little, and others more, but all returning more or less of that; then the dishes of the remaining prisoners would be empty. Those were the only days I counted so carefully in the spring, but judged them to be fair samples for that time of the year. But the number was not small who did not pretend to take this meal while the cracked wheat appeared. Then, as informed, they would pursue a similar course with certain other meals, for instance, when the fish was served. Some would not take the soup meal. The Sabbath morning repast of baked beans was ever spoken of as good, satisfactory both in quality and quantity. One man said his custom was to save some of the beans as a relish for his meals early in the week. The peas were complained of as bad. One overseer said to a prisoner, who was making his dinner of these, "I would as soon take so much shot into my stomach." The lack of vegetables was severely felt, especially that of onions, though I was informed they purchased a bushel, or so, in the winter, of very small onions, or scullions, as many call them. In the spring, I found a man in his cell sick, who said he was having symptoms of the scurvy, a difficulty he had in the army, that he was suffering much for the want of vegetables, and that he knew of others also suffering from these scurvy symptoms.

The warden, of course, well knew of this dislike of the food, but the men must take what he allowed or go without. A man asserted, on leaving prison, that the warden said to him, "All I have against you is, that you would not take your rations better." He replied, "I purposed to obey the prison rules, but did not feel myself bound to eat what I could not relish." One who was sick in his cell with a dispeptic difficulty, said he could not take brown bread as it soured on his stomach, but could eat white bread, for which he had asked, but to no purpose. I mentioned the matter to the steward, asking if he could not have the white bread. He answered, "No. They indulged him in that under the former administration and he thinks he must continue to have it, but now every one is to fare alike, so he must take his chance with the rest."

But the reader will ask, "Did not this warden allow the men who chose, to take anything extra?" Certainly. The former custom had been to place brown bread, cut in slices, near the rations, each man having the privilege of taking as many slices extra as he might choose. Or, he would convey dishes with extra rations to certain cells afternoons if requested, or when the occupants were to work extra evenings. This warden allowed any, desiring, to take of the brown bread extra, but only one slice each. I would now, also, though very seldom, see dishes of cracked wheat setting on the beds as extra rations, or basins of hash-skins.—The reader understands that, in making hash, more or less will dry, or burn upon the sides of the kettle, leaving a thick skin when all the eatable part is removed.—This skin, scraped from the kettle, composed these hash-skins, perfectly dry as husks. This was to save everything and have nothing wasted.—The reader will understand again, that when distributing books to the cells, and looking after the books, I could not avoid seeing these things.

With the failing flesh also went the strength to work. A man described the effect on himself, thus: "On first going into the shop after eating, I feel quite vigorous for my task, but soon a peculiar goneness comes on, and finally becomes so that what I do is through fairly driving my system." He had been very vigorous, able to go through almost anything, but what he had passed here proved sufficiently powerful to bring him down.

An overseer told me, that the men in his division became so weak that it required great effort on his part to keep some of them at their task, they being hardly able to stand up by their machines. But his duty forced him to keep them there as long as they could do anything, though a part became unable to accomplish more than one quarter of their ordinary work. His heart would really ache for the fellows.

It should be recollected that everything in the shop, but tending them, is done by machines, each operation having a machine for performing it, the business of the prisoners being to pass the articles to and from the respective workers. Hence, the amount of work turned out did not, of course diminish in proportion with the failing strength of the workmen, as must have been the case in the old method of hand planing, sawing, &c.

I subsequently learned that food would be carried into the shop for the suffering men, but I know not to what extent. At first mentioning, I thought that it could not have been done, and expressed the doubt, but my informer explained how, showing a perfectly feasible way.

The effect of the new system was plainly visible, too, on the health of the men. This, of course, could not be avoided. A man, who was very healthy, and vigorous to work when it commenced, ran through the winter into early spring when he began signally to fail, said he could not eat the rations any longer, and went without food of any amount, still constantly performing his task, till his system entirely broke down, and he was taken to the hospital for a drugging course, the doctor remarking to me that he had "failed with no apparent cause." I think the want of food was sufficient cause. Had he received proper care and suitable aliment, he would, doubtless, have been spared this sickness. I was informed that, when he was near death's door, he was pardoned, to die with his friends.

Another, who had fallen a victim to prison treatment and was in the last stages of consumption, said to me, "Had they used me as well when I was in health and able to work as they now do, I should not have been here at this time." Calling the next day, I learned that he had received pardon and been carried home, that he might die there. His stay, I learned, was very short.

How many of these pardons were granted in view of death, I never knew. They were gratifying to friends most certainly, but would make the prison mortality appear smaller than it really was. For, surely, if a man sickened in prison and received pardon as above, his demise should of right be set down as among the prison deaths.

A man came out in the spring, having been a prisoner one year; was well and robust when entering, but the ordeal of the winter brought on a rheumatic difficulty, so that towards its close he was really sick, and, as he remarked, solicited the warden for the privilege of laying off and doctoring a little, with the answer, "I know what the matter is with you, you wish to get rid of work; you can go to the shop;" and he was given no respite, nor was anything done for him while there. He went home so used up, that, as his father asserted, it did not seem that he could have lived at the prison but a few weeks longer. He revived, however, with home air and home treatment, worked considerably through the summer, but, as fall came on, had a return of the rheumatic trouble contracted in prison, with which he suffered many months, and died. A number of others, too, on their leaving, I found completely broken down, who were sent away to friends, or places of their usual abode, to be maintained by relatives or at public expense. A man, when leaving, said that he had there sometimes been forced to work, when so sick that five dollars a day would have been no temptation to him for thus laboring. One was reported to me as having been kept to his machine till fainting, and then carried to the hospital. One, with a consumptive difficulty, not able to work in the shop, was put in the cook-room to do what he could there, and kept at his task till, one Sabbath eve, he was taken to the hospital where he died the next Tuesday morning.

But why pursue this dark recital? All such management, of course, made the prison sickness appear less in the physician's account than the reality. It seemed fortunate to the men that the term of sentence to many so expired as to leave them under this rule but a comparatively short time.

In conversation with an overseer here, who had large experience, the idea was started as to how long time would be required for the system reigning at the prison this year to use up completely the number it commenced with, could all have been kept truly under its influence, with no respite or mitigation. His conclusion was some two years. Nor could I think he was much out of the way, that is, take the case as it bore on a large share.

The system left its legitimate effects on the minds of the inmates, aside from driving to insanity and idiocy, namely, irritability, angry feeling, or moroseness. Under the former rule, the men, when leaving, would generally express much gratitude towards officers and friends for the interest taken in their welfare, apparently filled with a hope and inspiration here gained, prompting them to strive for their own best good, from which no little advantage, to them, might be hoped. But under this rule, how different! Men fully admitting the justice of their sentence, and having come with the purpose of serving it out submissively, and with not a word of fault-finding, would go away complaining of the wrongs done them in the general prison fare, their hearts filled with bitter feelings, prompting them to execrate those from whom they had suffered these wrongs, and curse the State for putting such men in power over the prison. One who was so reduced that he found it a task to walk about, remarked, on leaving, "I have some accounts to settle with them over there" (meaning the warden and deputy), "and if I recover, I shall return to Concord and settle with them. I will have my pay unless they are the strongest." Some would leave with the feeling of *don't care* as to what course they should take.

What was said above as to losing flesh among the prisoners, should be taken with some exceptions. The cooks could manage to satisfy their demands of appetite. So also could those doing common chores. Some were naturally very small eaters, and some would eat all furnished them, however prepared. The females had such food as went to the warden's table, and, so far as I learned, what they needed, and ever appeared in good heart, except when sick.

A female prisoner, for some offence, was condemned to her cell for a week and to feed on the rations from the other part, which was held by her probably as a God-send rather than a punishment, for it gave the females the very opportunity desired for really seeing on what the men had to live. After this, when a woman left she was not slow in her declamations against the miserable fare of the men, and how they must of necessity suffer.

---

36. *Comparative prison order for the two years.* Some represent that the present warden found great abuses in the prison, all of which he has corrected. No doubt, this idea has quite extensively prevailed, and that interested parties have taken no little pains to extend the impression as widely as possible. Let us, then, look to the point with care, and give full credit for whatever has been gained in that direction.

The warden banished from the prison all bouquets and flowers, and talked of them in the most sneering manner, contending that the practice of presenting them to prisoners was the most outrageous wrong. He has put an end to all attendance, from the city, upon prison meetings of every class, except when he may give special invitation himself; has abolished all lecturing to the inmates by outsiders; and would have abolished the secular school, but for the persistent efforts of the chaplain; has ended the custom of having the female prisoners assemble with the males in the chapel Sabbath mornings for worship, requiring all moral efforts made for them to be put forth in their work room. He has also ended all funeral observances at the prison, cut off all distribution of religious tracts to the prisoners, and all trinkets or trinket-making in the cells, and has forbidden the receiving of presents from friends, excepting tobacco, &c.

If there were prison abuses in any or all of these, he has effectively corrected them, and should receive the full credit.

Then there were those two orders which he established in the shop, and he should be credited with whatever good they secured. The one was, that a man, meeting company in a door or pass-way, must turn and face the wall till they had passed, thus professedly not seeing them, though, before turning, he must have enjoyed the sight of all. The other rule was, that the men, when waiting for work, must stand at their machines, and by no means sit down.

In respect to account-keeping, no comparison can be made, for, previous to the service of this warden, the arrangement had been entered into for him to have no concern with that, the financial matters being attended to by an agent.

We come next to the behavior of the prisoners, the great point really to be looked at,—the one which outsiders, no doubt, always suppose to be meant, when reading or hearing about gains in prison order. In the chapel, with the most critical observation and careful weighing, I could not discover the slightest difference. The behavior was good, equally good at all times, in both years. So, also, in the hall, as far as my knowledge extended. As to the shop, I could not pretend to judge from personal observation, but an overseer, who served under both, gave me all needed information. He said, that he found it more difficult to keep order in his division the second year than during the first; that some were more excitable, revengeful, inclined to vent their spite on their machines, if nothing else; to throw those out of order and break things generally, costing him far greater effort to manage them. The uniform testimony of the men leaving prison has been in the same direction,—that they were more inclined to watch their overseers and take the advantage to commit little misdemeanors, as would naturally arise from this increased prompting to vent their ill-feelings.

So far as I learned, more contraband information was smuggled in during the second than the first year; certainly I heard it often alluded to. They would hint at outside matters that I knew nothing of, and in a way that showed considerable knowledge of them. Take an illustration: The day after Pike's nomination as governor, a prisoner said, half inquiringly, "Well, it seems that Pike is nominated." I could not say "No," in truth, and, from my position, was not allowed to say, "Yes." Hence I answered, in a joking way, "How much you think you know about the outside world;" to which he replied, "I do know. I had a paper brought me that very afternoon, before it was dry, giving an account of the whole proceedings. He will be elected, too, and we shall have different fare at the prison."—What one knew would be communicated to others, so, of course, this fact was generally understood among the inmates.

I have since learned, that, during the second year, a somewhat regular correspondence was carried on between the two wings, three couples, I think, thus making their arrangements for marriage, to be consummated shortly after their release. And the enjoyment to them was, that some of these letters were passed directly before the warden's face and eyes, without his notice.

One letter from the south wing was miscarried, and fell into his hands, for which the sender was locked up and thus gained the knowledge, above referred to, of the men's rations. But, nothing daunted at the fate of this missive, she prepared another and sent it before her release, or very soon after, which passed in safety. Besides this irregularity, parties in prison corresponded with those even out of the State, giving a pretty full account of the prison management, a friend of mine being shown quite a pile of these letters.

Hence, taking all things into account as to the deportment of the prisoners, we are forced to the conclusion that no improvement was secured the second year over the first, but rather a loss, that is, so far as I saw or heard.

The warden, of course, did his best towards preventing all prison abuses, for he considers himself a very smart prison officer, so shrewd that no prisoner can get the advantage of him. But he sometimes found more than his match. Some thought it not a very hard matter to "pull the wool over his eyes." The question has more than once been asked, "Is it possible that he can be so befogged?" Why not? He is an old man, between seventy and eighty, of great self-esteem, perhaps entering his dotage. If such a man be placed in so responsible a position, what may we expect?

---

37. *Good traits in the warden for prison service.* He possessed two most excellent and important traits for a prison officer. He was usually at his post, would be but seldom away and then only for a short time, but once, I think, for a few days, during the year. He would also be almost constantly looking after things himself, not leaving matters altogether to subordinates. True, some would complain of finding him in unsuspected and rather out-of-the-way places, but it taught them ever to be on the alert, ready for inspection at all times.

While, however, these traits, with a moderate share of judgment, would qualify one for running a steam engine, other and still higher and more important qualities are needed for managing a prison.

---

38. *Chaplain's inability to prevent knowing more or less of the prisoner's troubles and the prison management.* If the chaplain is alive to the prisoners' moral needs, their sorrows of heart and intent on affording the requisite advice, in searching for knowledge how to direct his words, he will often, of necessity, learn more of things in general than he desires. The case of the young man spoken of in Sec. 25, who had been in the solitary and gave this as an excuse for no lesson, is in point. He was making no complaint, but simply excusing himself. This plea, however, brought with it an idea that no little lack of prudence may have existed in a point of prison management, but of which I could not judge without knowing further circumstances. Thus there are numerous incidental ways by which knowledge will come to mind unbidden. Men, thinking themselves ill-treated, or who see others wronged, will speak of these things before he can stop them, and thus some knowledge of wrong, perhaps, is gained. For example: A man in his cell, no little excited, commenced: "How my blood boiled this afternoon at seeing them throw S., that sick man, on those timbers, and hurt him so." But just as soon as I saw his drift, I called out, "Hold on. You know I must not hear about that." Before I could stop him, however, enough was in the mind to raise the supposition that the feeble one was being abused, which idea subsequently received confirmation from the fact of his death.

39. *Secular school success.* My course was to commence at No. 120 and call at every cell in succession, where the inmate would engage in study, till arriving at No. 1, and then over again in regular order, being able, to "go the rounds," as we called it, about twice a week, each receiving my attention only so often.

I had quite a variety of exercises. Two commenced their alphabet, although some twenty-four years old. A number took reading in easy sentences, with spelling. Some thirty took arithmetic in its various stages, a few, as in the year previous, taking it up in review a while before leaving. A number in this branch made good proficiency, considering their disadvantages. Two took book-keeping, one doing but little, the other obtaining such a knowledge of the science as to prepare him to keep books passably well. But this was under difficulties. Having no blanks for practice, I obtained for him three large slates, one for day book and so on. But soon I found him with blanks all ruled. True, they were made of brown wrapping paper, on which he would write with a pencil. Asking no questions, I looked to his work as he pushed on with all energy and determination. No one could be more diligent.

One, having been a machinist, expressed a desire, a while previous to his liberation, for an opportunity to practice somewhat on mechanical drawing.

I obtained some patterns, carrying him one at a time. He would copy them with great exactness, and had been called on occasionally to draw working patterns for machinery in the shop. How lamentable that a man of his talents should go into service.

One took Latin, went through the grammar, and became able to read somewhat in the reader. He expressed a determination to obtain an education, when released, for which he was striving, when last heard from.

One, a house painter by trade, took arithmetic, and English grammar. He was quick to learn, and a keen, smart fellow. He frequently expressed the wish that he could learn something of ornamental painting, and thus be able to work on signs and fancy carriages, when liberated. I, of course, could do nothing for him at that, directly. But it occurred to me that perhaps I could, in a measure, indirectly. I could perhaps start him somewhat in penciling, thus leading his mind to a practical knowledge of making the sketches and outlines of what he would wish to paint. This idea he grasped with avidity, commencing, in a drawing-book that I furnished him, on simple outlines, thence to shading, and finally to foliage, showing as good improvement as is usually found in our schools. And this exhibited the more talent in him from the fact that I could give only a few general hints at the work, from what I had gathered by hearing teachers when directing their pupils. Hence, when coming to difficulties, he was left to work upon them as best he could, till conquered.

Having a work on Perspective, from which I had gained a few ideas, I gave him some hints on that. But we had nothing to practice upon but the inside of the prison, the walls and windows. He labored somewhat on the idea of the vanishing point, and that of the diminution of the angle of vision as distance increases.

Thus, the reader will see, our school took a somewhat wide range. I would interest the mind, so far as could be, in what would profit, and thus beget a love for truth and turn the attention away from wrong. With the wholesome ideas gathered in these studies, I would also inculcate the moral, to elevate the thoughts and heart to the truly good. Here, I constantly kept in view the idea of the best interest of the prisoner and the State.

This labor was most fatiguing. Standing there at the cell doors with no means of sitting, I would, at times, become so completely exhausted as to be obliged to retire to rest a while. Then, taking the air from the cells would occasionally be most repulsive and injurious to health, the whole weakening to the system.

I attempted to have a short school exercise with the females twice a week, but word soon came that they could not be spared for that, and the effort was abandoned. The pupils did as much, perhaps, as could rationally be expected, under the circumstances. Could we have had the school in the chapel, greater results would have crowned our efforts, with much less labor.

Though I was wholly cut off at first from having an evening school in the chapel, near the latter part of January, the warden informed me that I might have one there on Thursday evenings, if I would give up the prayer meeting, but not to begin till warmer weather. I could not harbor the idea, for a moment, of relinquishing the prayer meeting, and supposed I must wait for the proposed Thursday evening effort till the warden moved. At length, I found that he was waiting for me, when it was too late to move in the matter at all. Indeed, had we attempted the effort when first spoken of, it would probably have been more trouble than benefit.

As to the penciling, nothing was said by any in disapprobation of it, yet, after that hearing, with the thought that possibly this might be one of the points of offense, I took from him all the materials except, perhaps, the slip on perspective, which he greatly regretted.

---

40. *Sabbath school success.* The prison year commences the first of May. The former warden continued some ten weeks into the second year, during which time the Sabbath school attendance remained as usual, averaging eighty-six.

On the first Sabbath of the new order nearly the same number were in attendance. But many had no teachers provided, and I could have nothing to do about arranging for the school's best interest.[4] The following Sabbath brought a great falling off, still greater the next, and so on. In a few weeks the warden peremptorily dismissed one of the teachers he had invited, telling him that if he would call at another time, he would give his reason.

[4] In speaking of the Sabbath school teachers employed, page 69, the author intended to say, such a number that each teacher could have a guard stand by him and see that nothing contraband passed.

At first, a prisoner would occasionally ask a question, as usual, and a little discussion spring up; but the warden at once crushed all this, requiring the teachers simply to put the questions as in the book and the pupil to give the answer and nothing more. The number continued to fall off until it went below thirty, giving me fears that none would attend, all my efforts for their continuance being of no avail. No excuse would usually be given. But one said, "I won't attend with such a warden," and I judged this the general reason. At length I found uneasiness pervading the teachers, one having determined to resign; but I entreated him to remain for the sake of the prisoners and the Sabbath school, for, if he left, his class would follow, dropping the number to twenty or under, and all would be likely to take the same course. He did not feel satisfied with laboring under such circumstances, with a guard, may be a mere boy, at his side to watch him, and he, perhaps, turned off as unceremoniously as the other. He preferred going of his own accord. But my plea prevailed, and he remained.

The average attendance after the advent of the new order was forty-eight; for the whole year, fifty-seven.

---

41. *Religious success.* The contrast between the religious element of the present year and that of the past was painful. Still, among those who at first gave up all hope of struggling against the tide, a few were induced to forsake that ground and struggle on; thus we hope something of the past was saved.

In my discourses I felt impelled to dwell more largely on the moral code, to which the inmates gave respectful attention. The prayer meetings were well attended, though but few of the inmates would take any part. One of the Sabbath school teachers was usually present, and labored with good effect. We took up more of the time in Bible exposition, which would occasionally seem to awaken some interest.

As to our true religious success this year, or the real good accomplished, none but that Being who knows all things can decide. One thing is certain, much earnest, prayerful effort to that end was made, much hard labor performed. But it is difficult rowing against wind and tide. Still, we probably shared in as large success as could reasonably be looked for under all the circumstances.

---

42. *Lack of truthfulness at the prison.* We are often told that no confidence can be placed in the word of a prisoner. But in my experience under the new rule, I was taught the sad lesson that I could place no greater confidence in the assertions of some of the officers. A complaint of this character had repeatedly been made by released prisoners. Still, it required personal experience to enable me to appreciate its full and lamentable force. Hence, the shock I felt at the virtual request of the warden for me to join in the falsehood course, by telling the prisoners that Henry Stewart, when removed to the insane asylum, was taken out to be tried for attempts to murder his overseer.—Then, again, there were the assertions I repeatedly heard the warden make to prison visitors, on passing through the cook-room. "We give the prisoners good food and enough of it. We purchase the best of articles the market affords, and have the food well prepared." He

would repeat this in earnestness and apparent sincerity, as though he really believed it himself.—Subsequently, a gentleman of the city, of undoubted veracity, being about to visit the parents of a prisoner, called and asked the warden how he was, with the answer, "He is all right; you may tell his folks that he is all right." In a few days after, it was found that, at the very time of this assertion, the man was so sick that the doctor had nearly given him over to die.

Then I would sometimes smile and sometimes feel sorrowful at his changeable appearance; perhaps if one of influence and authority came in, he would put on peculiar airs of suavity, and expatiate upon how things were and should be in prison, while one without that influence might enter and receive entirely different treatment. I here see how our rulers may have been led on at times, unaware of the true state of things in the institution. How easy to cover up!

Then in the female department, I called for a convict in order to arrange for her disposal on leaving prison, and was told, "The assistant is in the city with the key to their apartment, therefore you can not see the woman." But how was I surprised shortly to learn that, at the moment of this assertion, the assistant was in the kitchen at work, and known to be there by my informant.

Is it any wonder that such people disbelieve in prison reform?

---

43. *Reported quarrel between the warden and chaplain.* The idea has been circulated, how extensively I know not, that the warden and chaplain had a quarrel between them at the prison. It seems to have pervaded some minds in the legislature at Concord in '71, being used to the disadvantage of a bill before that body in regard to the prison, the fate of which perhaps was made to turn on that. No doubt a certain Concord gentleman, who had an ax of his own to grind in connection, knows very well how this report was made so prevalent. Whether he or another started it, I know not.

But that idea had not the slightest foundation in truth. The circumstances of our official intercourse in all that passed, have been faithfully set forth in the preceding pages, and the reader can see for himself that there was no quarreling. When the warden told me to "bring the key back and not touch it any more," I did as required, without uttering a word. When I told him what I should do about fixing up the Maine man before sending him away, his remark was in no fault-finding tone. When he pointed out my work at first, and in our connected colloquy, all our words were civil and courteous, no unpleasantness in tone; and when he informed me on the point of the man's glasses and the sick man's flannels, I gave him no unkind answer.

And where was the quarreling? Nowhere. It did not exist. He taught me my bounds after the manner he did, and I accepted them and conformed my moves thereto with not a lisp of fault-finding. He never spoke a word in disapprobation of what I was doing, but that all was agreeable to his mind. Again, where was that place of quarreling? Not in the prison between the warden and chaplain. Whenever we met, it was on the most civil terms, we invariably passing the compliments of the day.

True, we each had our notions on prison reform, he thinking that attempts in that direction are useless, that, when one has fallen into prison we can not reform him, that punishment is *the* great mission of the prison, and thus on; I, supposing that reform is practicable, that we should faithfully use all available means for it, and make it the paramount object of imprisoning. On the question of prison order we were exactly alike in sentiment,— perfect order, strict discipline,—though, perhaps, varying as to the ultimate results, he securing that as a deterrent to crime; I, as an important and indispensable element in reform, leading the once erring to that state of mind in which he will hate wrong and love right.

Then, as we had not a word of debate over our differing ideas, so there was no clashing in carrying them out. The warden established his line of policy, as he had a legal right, then I surveyed the ground and decided to go on with my reform efforts, so far, with respect to time and place, as I could consistently with his arrangements, at all times looking to the best prison order, and at no time to interfere with any of his moves.

This was our prison quarreling, and the whole of it; a very peaceful affair. How happy, if all quarrels were of this character! I felt assured that, though what I was endeavoring to promote in our prison was held by those at present in the ascendant as being an interloper in such an institution, and wholly out of place there, truth would at length prevail. Prudent labors, persevering efforts, patient waiting and firm trust in the great Leader, would now, as ever before, result in the triumph of the right. With such views I daily toiled in quietness, interfering with nobody around me.

———————

44. *Prison Report for '71.* I had looked for a pretty free use of whitewash in this, but it goes immeasurably beyond my anticipations. I really expected to find some regard for truthfulness in the statement of facts. But, in my astonishment at reading, I would inquire, "Have I fallen into a general confusion of names? Is black indeed white?"

Let us read, p. 13,—"He [the warden] ... spends his whole time in and about the institution, not having been absent to the value of half a day since he entered upon his duties."

Thus we have it. Sum up the time spent by the warden during the year in going to the P. O., or in calls out on business, or errands, or attending meeting on the Sabbath, or journeying to New York even, and the whole does not amount to "the value of half a day." This prepares us for any statement we may find. If we admit that, we can anything.

Let us, then, look at the food question.

On page 6. we have,—"The food furnished the prisoners has been selected with more than ordinary care and great pains have been taken in having it well cooked and served. We have a regular weight from which the rations are made, and any man, wishing for more than the regular allowance, is always furnished with an extra quantity." P. 13,—"The warden is not only valuable as a disciplinarian but is economical in his management of the affairs of the prison, at the same time allowing to the prisoners liberal rations of food of the best quality, but none to waste."

This can be admitted just as easily as the quotation preceding. How rejoiced the prisoners would have been to realize the truthfulness of this assertion one short week,—"Selected with more than ordinary care!" "Regular weight!" "Liberal rations of food of the best quality!" That will do,— decaying fish, potatoes "not fit to put into the human stomach," and all.

But when the Report comes to the chaplain it uses a black wash with quite as unsparing a hand, thus, (P. 13) "But the warden has not had that sympathy and assistance from the chaplain, which should be mutually rendered to each other by officers of the prison. The chaplain, for reasons best known to himself, has not acted in harmony with the warden in the discharge of his various duties, a matter very essential to the discipline of a prison. He has on the other hand, manifested peculiarities of his own which have been very detrimental to the discipline, and, we have reason to believe, have caused some uneasiness among the prisoners, which has made it more difficult for the warden, and, in some instances, causing punishment which would otherwise have been avoided."

But let us read what the warden says (P. 9),—"In conclusion, I desire to express my thanks to all the officers connected with the institution, for the prompt, cheerful and efficient manner in which they have discharged their several duties."

The chaplain was one of those officers. What, then, shall we believe? Who tells the truth? What has become of straightforward dealing? Where is that trait once called honor among men? The reader, having fully informed himself of the real facts, will pronounce the above charge against the chaplain as unqualifiedly untrue from beginning to end.

But one says, "That first assertion must be true. The warden could not have shared your sympathy in his acts." No, that first assertion is not true. It is equally false with all the rest, that is, in the sense of the writer, which evidently is that the chaplain did not sympathize with the warden in his desires for order, and labor with him to that end. Order is the first thing to be sought in prison as everywhere else. It has my fullest sympathy and for the very purpose of helping towards it, under this warden, I voluntarily undertook what I did.

"The warden has not had that assistance from the chaplain," &c. The reader has seen the chaplain putting in a pacific word here and there, doing all he could to interest the mind in its privations, helping men keep down their angry passions, robbing the solitary of its occupants, excusing, entreating, helping to order in every way possible, and is held up in that light.

"Not acted in harmony." Not a discordant word or step is the truth.

"Manifested peculiarities of his own." Peculiarities! What were they? Honest devotion to duty and not an eye to personal popularity; most arduous toils engaged in for helping to the best interest of the prison; patient efforts for reforming and elevating the fallen. All I said or did there would come within some of these points. Were those peculiarities? What then must be the character of the prison management? If the chaplain's moves were held as peculiarities it could have been only from contrasting the animus and acts of those who ruled with his. They would hold the prisoners as so many "dumb, driven cattle;" he, as human beings, with instincts of reason to be addressed and emotions of right to be stirred; they, in all cases, would move their brute fears, threaten, scold, drive; he, a part of the time at least, would appeal to the manhood sentiments, persuade, entreat, expostulate; they would regard them as morally hopeless, to be cruelly treated, and made money of; he, as those for whom hope lives, and on whom redeeming influences should be used, and efforts made for coining from them gold purer than earth affords.

Nor are these moves of the chaplain peculiarities in many other States, if in N. H. Nor are they original with him. Other minds had brought out such ideas and pushed them somewhat widely into public acceptance, and he was only attempting to introduce something of their benign influence here.

"Detrimental to discipline." What gross darkness!

"Made it more difficult for the warden." Change "difficult" to "easy" and the truth would be told.

"Causing punishment." What an idea!

The chaplain saw the changes attempted to be brought upon the prisoners, and thought he understood something of the effects which the move would produce on their minds and the results likely to follow. He knew that to some extent he had the confidence of the men, that they were looking to him as their friend, and as working for their best good; that, therefore, he could, by carefully using his influence in a quiet, unassuming way, help slide the matters round the very sharp corner which was being turned, and thus, on the one hand, make things more endurable to the inmates, and, on the other, easier for the rulers. With an eye single to this purpose he acted, and has the satisfaction of possessing pretty clear evidence that he prevented a measure of trouble in the prison, and thus rendered the warden some aid at least, and made his task somewhat easier. Indeed, he did what he could in that direction, though with no blowing of trumpets. And, after doing all this, to be held up in this light by the agent is a pretty hard cut.

Now, one of two things is true in regard to all the quotations above made. The assertors either believed they were telling the truth or they did not. If the former be taken, if they really thought they could purchase the articles they did and from them make the best quality of food; if they really supposed the chaplain's moves were as deleterious as they represent, what does it show in regard to their judgment as fitting them for place and trust? or, if the other, what of their character as to truth and veracity? Let them take which horn of the dilemma they may choose.

One perhaps says, "The writers were so informed about the chaplain." Could that be any extenuation of their wrong? If such insinuations had been made to them, why did they not first give some intimation of it to him, thus giving him the opportunity of showing their falsity? Why did they not have the parties face to face, and thus learn the truth? But, instead of this, they published what they did, and that to the injury of an innocent man, so far as their influence could go.

But what could have impelled the assertors to such a course? The author does not pretend to know, but it looks as though the object was in this way to push the chaplain to resign, and they thus be rid of those reform efforts. Hence p. 13,—"The prison is a penal institution, and is intended for punishment, not primarily as a reformative one, as some people think." Here is, undoubtedly, the key to this raid on the chaplain. But what is its full import? These reformers fully believe that the sentence of the court must be strictly carried out, and that, too, as an element of reform. The above sentence must mean that the prisoner is put there to be punished as the State directs by its laws and courts, and, in addition, for the managers to "use him so that he will not wish to come back," or to punish him as they may choose. If the sentence means anything, it must mean that. This being the true way, let us have it so understood, and, next summer, let the legislature recognize the idea by a specific act, and then let the judge change his sentence accordingly, putting it, "Your sentence is, that you be confined at hard labor in the State Prison at Concord for —— years, and that you there be further punished at the discretion of the prison officers acting for the time being." Let this be announced to all evildoers; and, further, let the warden, agent and all, give a true account of the severity of their several punishments, to be published yearly, that the prison may thus appear as deterring to crime as possible. Away with this covering up and pretending to the best living and best usage generally, thus making the institution appear so attractive. A lady visited a friend there and returned, having been made, by the warden's palaver, perfectly reconciled to the friend's condition, remarking, "They are kept so well there, and used so kindly, that one can not feel bad at all about a friend in the prison, except from the fact that he can not have his liberty to go out as he chooses." I protest against such proceedings. But let the truth stand forth, just as it is, that the wicked may really know upon what they must depend.

Why not put out the sentiment squarely that reform moves have no place in the prison? Let us be truthful in this, too. Then dismiss the chaplain and save that expense to the State, for he can be of no use.

It is made evident that the writers would banish from prison all reform moves from this assertion, p. 13,—"We think, sometimes, the matter of reform or sympathy for the prisoners is carried so far, in attempting to reform, as to lead the prisoners to believe that they are injured persons instead of transgressors, which is, in our opinion, wrong, and has a bad tendency." Is not the writer here a little muddled? or would he hold up these reformers as so absurd a set as to think of reforming men by making them believe they are good already and really sinned against? Indeed, would not the labors of such men of straw be bad? True, the writer pretends to found his objections to the reform efforts on the fact that they are carried too far, not perhaps, feeling exactly ready, at this late day, to come out squarely against efforts to raise the fallen, and to induce the erring to become good citizens. No, but it is "carrying the matter too far." Just as though we could go too far in efforts for saving the drowning man. Away with such a sham!

This indirect charge must have been aimed at the chaplain, for he was the only prison officer, that year, who could rightly be accused of such a crime as attempting reform moves.

We are again told that Mr. P. had brought the institution to where it was "with firmness, but with kindness and a Christian spirit," which unfolds the writer's views of "kindness" and the "Christian spirit." No doubt the prisoners were just wicked enough to say, "Lord, deliver us from all such 'Christian spirit.'"

We are further assured, that Mr. P. "has accomplished wonders in this direction, for, in our view, there is now no better disciplined prison in the N. E. states."

That is a very comfortable feeling, very much more so than the emotions of some, who, going into others States, are made to blush at the taunts thrown out about our prison management, that "such things will do for you N. H. folks, for those so far on the background."

But let us turn to the financial part of the Report. Long before the document made its appearance, it had been heralded far and wide in the papers that those now running the prison had made it produce a clear gain of over five thousand dollars in nine months. Of course, making this announcement was for personal popularity. Let us look at the figures after the Report comes to hand. Number of prisoners, 85 males and 6 females. Profits reported for nine months and twenty days, $5173.51, including $396.65 paid on roofing shop. Without deducting this item, we have $5570.16 gain over the real running expenses, which, for a whole year, would amount to $6914.67. Let us compare this with the gain of the Massachusetts State Prison for '72, that Report being at hand. Its number of inmates were 543. If our 91 prisoners gained what they are represented, then 543, in that proportion, would gain $41,260.06, without considering the advantage in larger numbers. Reckoning that in, it would raise this gain to some $45,000, no doubt, the gain of Massachusetts in proportion to ours. But what was her gain? It was $14,635.23, ours being, in proportion, more than three times as much as hers, we thus leaving her all out of sight.

The writers say, p. 11, in regard to Mr. P., "His management has been perfectly satisfactory to your committee. The results of his administration are the most conclusive proofs of its efficiency." Do any wonder that the committee should be satisfied with such showing, if looking to nothing but to the dollars and cents?

But does not the announcement itself show an aggravated wrong to the prisoners, or a false representation? It must be one or the other, if not both. There is no possible way to accomplish all this by honest shrewdness in financiering and rightful treatment to the convicts. All articles of food have their market value. If really suitable for use, the value is fixed for the time being, from which no material deduction can be had. Things have their wholesale and retail prices. True, these vary more or less, from accidental causes, such as the abundance or scarcity of the article, the state of the money market, or the season of the year. Buyers, by watching these accidental influences, may purchase more or less to their advantage. And one can look to these points, and profit from them, as well as another. Prison providers, especially in large establishments, will purchase, of course, at wholesale, and those at Charlestown enjoy quite as good advantages, to say the least, for sharing in these accidentals as those at Concord; and they no doubt look out quite as shrewdly. If, however, one is willing to turn from articles fit for use, he can find those as cheap as he desires, going down from thirteen cents to three or one, if he likes.

Then this boast of great gains at our prison gives a suspicious look, to say the least. If we allow for all that cruel cutting off, previously depicted, and even more, that would not bring the accounts to what would appear probable. The agent, in purchasing legitimate articles, manifested no skill beyond others. He certainly ran behind on wood as as I happened to learn by experience. The man who furnished the prison with this, agreed to supply some for me, of the same quality and price, but failed to bring it at the time, which forced me to look elsewhere for what I needed and which I found, with no extra painstaking and at a bargain, reckoning price and quality, better by one dollar at least per cord.

But if this withholding from the prisoners what they so greatly needed and what was their just due, will not bring the accounts within the region of probability, to what source shall we look for the discrepancy? Let us examine the accounts carefully and see what we thus find. True, it is said, "Figures won't lie," but men, when disposed, may so use them as to lead wide of the truth. In our examination we find the same dealing as before pointed out. Important items of expense in running the institution are deliberately omitted in reckoning. Thus, there is the warden's salary of $1000, the chaplain's, $750, printing the Report, $121,98, appraisers', $78, amounting to $1949,98. Subtracting this from the pretended gain, $6914,67 - 1949,98, gives 4964,69. Let us see what this would be with the Charlestown number of men, $29,625,56, over two times the comparative gain at Charlestown, a very large margin to be accounted for in our withholding.

Certainly we can not afford to boast very loudly over these figures, but should rather blush. The reader should bear in mind, that the prisoners are let at both places on contract, ours at ninety cents per day, and those in Massachusetts for over one dollar, so that her prison managers enjoy an advantage over ours for rolling up gains. And when we talk of gaining more than twice as much as she, we have reason to fear that those hearing us will say, that too many of those dollars were ground out of the flesh, and blood, and sinews, and life even of the prisoners,—not a very welcome sentiment.

45. *Efforts of the Prison Aid Association for legislation in favor of the prison.* The Governor, in his message of '69, proposed that the prison be put under the management of a Board especially appointed to that purpose. But, instead of this, and in connection, making such other provisions for the institution as were really needed, the legislature simply passed the whole matter over into the hands of the Governor and Council, as this Board, an improvement somewhat, no doubt, over the former system, but an arrangement, which, in the views of many of our best citizens, carries with it grave objections.

The Board, thus constituted, is a changeable body, the members never remaining in office more than two years, and sometimes but one. As a result, the prison must necessarily be managed largely by the inexperienced, for the men, generally, no doubt, come to the office without having given any special attention to the subject. This is much like setting a company of untaught landsmen to navigate a ship.

Again, the prison is liable to no little changeableness in its mode of being directed, a great detriment to its welfare, unless it be from bad to good. Men will possess their varying notions, and some, though lacking a knowledge of the best prison interests, will persist in having their peculiar views put in practice, however conflicting and contradictory. It is also now liable to be left largely in the hands of the warden to be run as he wills, besides being exposed to the unfavorable effects of political party influence. Finally, the institution can receive only its part of the largely divided attention of its managers, and thereby, at times, be liable to inconvenience.

But the best interest of the prison evidently demands the control of men especially adapted to their task, men who shall form a body with all possible permanence, possess ripe experience, be free in their rule from partisan control, who shall make the institution their speciality, and manage after some fixed policy involving the most enlightened principles, principles of true reform.

The Association took up these matters, and for the purpose of obtaining legislation looking as undividedly in this direction as possible, appointed a committee, of which Rev. Mr. Sanborn of Concord served as chairman, who should, after due investigation and correspondence with other States, prepare the requisite bill for legislative consideration. After much labor, the following, as subsequently amended, was presented to the legislature at its session in '71.

STATE OF NEW HAMPSHIRE.

IN THE YEAR OF OUR LORD ONE THOUSAND EIGHT HUNDRED AND SEVENTY-ONE.

An act in relation to the Penal Institutions.

Be it enacted by the Senate and House of Representatives in General Court convened:

SECTION 1. There shall be a Board of directors of Prisons to consist of five persons appointed by the Governor, by and with the advice and consent of the Senate, who shall hold office for five years, except that the five first appointed shall hold their office for 1, 2, 3, 4 and 5 years respectively, the commission of each designating his term of office. Thereafter one Director shall be appointed annually in the month of June, to hold his office five years. Such Board shall have charge and superintendence of the State Prison, and shall have such power, and perform such duties in respect to County Jails, the Reform School and other penal and reformatory institutions within the State, as the Legislature may by law impose upon it. The Board may, from time to time, elect from its own members or otherwise, a Secretary, who shall perform such duties as the Board may prescribe, and shall receive such salary as the Legislature may determine. The other members of the Board shall receive no compensation, other than reasonable and other traveling expenses, while engaged in the performance of official duty. And the limit of such expenses shall be in amount —— to each individual, which shall not be changed except at intervals of five years.

SECTION 2. Such Board shall have power,

I. To appoint the Warden, Deputy Warden, Chaplain, Physician and Surgeon of the State Prison, and shall have power to remove either of such officers, for cause only, after opportunity to be heard in his own defense upon written charges. All other officers and guards of the prison shall be appointed by the Warden thereof, and shall be removable at his pleasure.

II. To define the powers, duties and compensation of such officers, except the compensation of the Warden.

III. To establish by-laws for the government of the prison.

IV. To provide for the purchase of all articles necessary for the use of the prison, or the health and comfort of the officers and prisoners.

V. To provide for the sale of all articles manufactured in the prison or not needed for the use thereof.

VI. To make contracts, if expedient, for the support and employment of the prisoners or any portion of them.

VII. To make all necessary additions, alterations and repairs within the prison or its inclosure.

VIII. To provide such books and instruction as may be considered necessary for the convicts.

IX. To draw its warrant through its Secretary upon the State Treasurer in favor of the Warden for all appropriations made by the Legislature for the State Prison.

SECTION 3. Such Board shall visit the State Prison at least once every month, and oftener, when thought necessary, for the purposes of ascertaining whether the laws, rules and regulations are faithfully observed.

SECTION 4. The Governor may remove either of the Directors of the Prison for malfeasance or misfeasance in office, after having furnished him with a copy of the charges against him, and giving him an opportunity to be heard in his own defense.

SECTION 5. All acts and parts of acts, inconsistent with this act, are hereby repealed, and this act shall take effect from and after its passage.

This bill was presented and went to the judiciary committee of the House, a body composed of two ex-judges and other gentlemen of influence, all of whom favored it, some saying to me, privately, that it was the very thing needed. The committee reported it unanimously. It passed the House with no opposition, and so also the Senate, the final vote having been taken when some private interest in Concord started up to defeat the measure and induced a member of the Senate to move a reconsideration of that vote. His move prevailed, and the bill was referred back to the Senate committee, before which this interest appeared in objection to the measure, while friends were present in its advocacy. The committee again reported unanimously in favor of the passage of the document, but on taking final action it was postponed to the next session of the legislature.

Here was the point where the story circulated of the warden and chaplain quarrel, that this bill was the embodiment of certain peculiar notions of the latter which he was pushing to the disadvantage of the former, muddling some of the Senate, and thus leading them to think it not best to be "mixed up in the matter," and so to vote that the measure be put over.

It is wonderful to think how slight an influence will sometimes thwart an important measure in passage at the legislature. A mere whisper of some whim, a little prejudice against another, perhaps may put it all aside. How little attention is given to merit! This is true even of Hon. Senators. To one of these I spoke about his vote within ten minutes after he had given it, and he replied,—"I don't know, I am sure, how I voted, for I did not care anything about it."

The fact is, this bill did not originate with me. I had nothing to do with it, not being on the committee who framed it. But, as Agent of the Association, I spent more or less time at the State House, looking after the interest of the measure.

The next session the bill came up in the Senate again, and, through the same interest as before, probably, it was indefinitely postponed and another put on passage in its stead, which went to the House committee on prisons. But they did not think it worthy of being reported, and that died. A member of the committee remarked that it appeared to be a scheme started by one for the purpose of making a comfortable place for himself. And he, no doubt, had the right of it, for the prominent provision was that the Board should consist of three, one of whom must be a resident of Concord, and not be allowed over four hundred dollars. That would be a nice thing for the Concord man. Thus matters stand at present so far as legislation is concerned.

If the reader will give attention to the bill above presented, he will see that it is very comprehensive, and might easily be carried out. It contemplates the needed permanence, each member being in long enough to obtain large experience in prison management, yet changing sufficiently often to avoid the ill effect of remaining in office too long. It further contemplates small expenses, as each member of the Board is to charge nothing for his time.

It has been suggested that the bill be further amended, by striking out the words "and other instruction," in Article VIII., and inserting the following Section after Sec. 3, thus, Section 4: This Board shall consider the reform of the prisoners the paramount object of the prison, and shall secure to them such secular, Sabbath school, moral and religious instruction as, in their view, shall be most conducive to this end, but not therein to conflict with the labor interests of the institution.

One objects to the above bill, that, as it proposes no compensation for the time spent by the members of the Board, men of efficiency can not be found to act upon it. If the concern is to be run simply for money-making, that would be the fact; and of right should be. But, when we come to labors for raising these fallen ones from their crimes and degradation to uprightness and a higher life, in a word, to make true men and women of them as we ought, it is quite another thing. In that case we have men, good and true, men fully qualified for the task; men who, while carrying out the primary objects of the prison,—good order, good discipline and true reform every way,—would also present the best truthful show of legitimate gains in dollars and cents. Certainly it is demeaning to our State to think otherwise. We have men among us, of noble minds and large hearts, who, by honest industry and true integrity of purpose, have raised themselves to that position in the public estimate where they deservedly share the fullest confidence of their fellows, for ability and fidelity to the highest and purest aims, and who feel that they owe it as a gratuity to society to lend a measure of their talents in managing her public interests. Hence, no difficulty is found in obtaining men to act with the highest efficiency as trustees to our colleges and seminaries without compensation. So, too, enough can be found really fitted to run the prison as proposed.

Another objection to the bill has been, that it does not make it obligatory for one of the Directors to reside in Concord. As the object of the legislation is for the special advantage of the prison, rather than to make a place for a certain Concord gentleman, it was not thought needful to insert such a limitation. Then, again, railroad facilities are so great as to do away with the need of such an enactment. That whole matter can be safely left in the hands of the appointing power, who should look for the best men to the position.

But the bill, with the connected ideas, is here placed before the reader, with the ardent hope that it will be thoroughly studied by him, improved where it can be, or a better one substituted, and thus the best system of prison management practicable be hit upon and made a law as soon as may be, thereby running the institution on principles commensurate with the prevailing intelligence of our people, the genius of our Christian civilization, and in keeping with the times in which we live and what is being accomplished in other States.

---

46. *Experience with the new government.* In June, '71, the Democratic rule gained the ascendency at Concord. When the new rulers became established in their places, and were able to give attention to prison matters, the Governor sent for me to call at the council chamber, which I did. His desire, as well as that of his council, was to know really about the state of things at the prison. It seemed that statements had been made to them tending to show something of their true character. I gave some general intimations as I understood matters, but could not, from the circumstances, enter into particulars as on the preceding pages; and, indeed, had not then so learned some of the facts that I was at liberty to speak of them. They professed a determination to have the prisoners properly treated, with enough to eat and of good food, though the Governor said he had not posted himself on prison matters at all, not thinking it worth while from the circumstances. It will be understood that he was elected, not by the popular vote, but by the legislature, and, previous to its assembling, he could put but little confidence in his election there.

---

47. *Chaplain determines to have an investigation into the charges against him in the Prison Report, but relinquishes the idea.* On reading the Prison Report for that year, I felt not only shocked at the character of its general statements, so far as the warden and committees were concerned, but also determined on having an investigation into the charges against me. Touching one's character in that way is no trifling matter, and I did not feel like sitting quietly down under representations so entirely false. Had I been guilty, I would have borne the deserved rebuke without a murmuring word. Some proposed that the new Governor and Council make a general investigation of the prison matters, and I put this in with the rest. But they were not inclined to that unless parties preferred charges, in which case they would hear and consider them. Hence, I decided to call for a hearing on those allegations, and prepared the papers according to legal advice, but thought best, before sending them in, to consult certain influential friends in the place about attempting the move, and received a decided remonstrance against it; they arguing that the step would stir up strife, make divisions and party alienations; that, in the uncertainty of things, I had no assurance of obtaining satisfaction, and the like. Supposing this to be given in sincerity, and that, perhaps, it might be for the best, I gave the matter up, and threw aside my papers.

---

48. *Anniversary of P. A. Association for '71 and remarks on our jails.* This was held in the Representatives' Hall, at Concord, the second Tuesday evening of June. Ex-Gov. Smyth, President in the chair. Attendance not large. The Agent gave a full report of the past year's doings, showing that good success had attended their efforts, and that the enterprise was taking hold of the public mind in a measure, though with some opposition. It had been a year of planning, commencing and going forward as a new struggle in the State; the object of the Association being to aid those released from prison by furnishing them with good, immediate employment, under proper influences and with suitable surroundings, helping with money only as indispensable, and then not intrusting it to those aided to disburse. An important beginning had been made, much hard work performed, and a measure of good evidently accomplished, giving favorable indications for the future, with the needed energy and effort. Only $100.50 of the $300 appropriated by the State had been expended.

In preparing this Report, the Agent had written to all the jails in the State, proposing over thirty questions for answers, in order to develop the state of crime and the penal working in our commonwealth. Only a part responded, but enough to furnish us with important subjects for study and effort. The good of society, the welfare of the State, loudly call for our better minds, our more influential workers to give most earnest attention to these matters. We should here make a great effort for improvement; an effort entered into by ministers of religion and those of justice, legislators and all. Woman, also, should come to the help.

As now managed our jails are prolific schools of crime. The old, hardened offender and the young, in comparative innocence, are huddled together, the latter to be taught in deeds of wrong and adroit methods of performing them of which he had never dreamed before; instruction that, perhaps, fires his mind to enter these ways of sin as a business for life. Does not this look to the need of a classification, in these institutions, that we now have not?

In some cases the women's cells are in the same wards with the men's, and they can freely talk together, though locked in separately, and probably never allowed to associate further. But there is a living remembrance of wrong, daily seen in Concord, which should cause us to blush, in the person of an unfortunate boy, who had his birth in jail, the mother having been in durance there one year previously as a candidate for State Prison,— another sad lesson for comment and remedial labors.

Our jails are cultivators of indolence. Men, women and children are locked in there with no useful employment,—except in that at Manchester,— nothing to do but to impart and study lessons of crime; and some manage to remain there the most of the time, preferring this to honest labor. These all go to swell the burdens of the tax-payer. Why not have some sort of industries connected with these places? Set these fellows at work on something. Keep them out of idleness, so far as can be. If the employment does not bring in largely of dollars and cents, it will, in what may be better. And are not some of our jails themselves nuisances, a disgrace to the State?

We need, at least, two work-houses. They may not be of great expense at ornamenting, but appropriate, substantial, fitted every way to their use. Then fill them with this vagabond population now floating back and forth between the establishments catering to vice and the jails. Give them really corrective sentences. Modify essentially this short-time-sentence system. If one's wrong habits are not corrected by one sentence, let the next be longer, or till thoroughly reformed, reform being the object aimed at. Then should we take the keepers of these rum-shops, billiard-saloons, gambling-dens and houses of ill-fame, with those of their frequenters that need be, and put them here at work, too. This would be a wonderful purifier of society. Give each a dose, say of six months, when, if that don't cure, repeat it till the work is accomplished in them also.

Then, here are numerous other connected questions for us to study, discuss and settle in regard to securing a general punitive system, a system in advance of what we now possess, more corrective of crime. And what shall be done for those children coming up in idleness, ignorance and vagrancy?

49. *Fourth of July at the prison in '71.* The observance this year was in exact contrast with that of last, the one bringing gratification and pleasure, the other, gloom and punishment. The workmen and other help desired prison work to cease that day, for their enjoyment, which was granted. But, instead of studying any means for giving a moment's pleasure to the inmates, they were locked in their cells for the day. But I spent the hours with them, going from cell to cell, and making efforts for removing the intolerable tedium, not unfrequently hearing the contrast between the last Fourth and this, alluded to with deep sighs. It would have been great relief to them could they have continued their work in the shop for the day. Hence, the remark of one and another, "How cruel to keep us shut up here!" "Oh, how much more agreeable to be out at work!" "I would rather work four times as hard as usual than be confined here." Thus, they expressed themselves. If punishment was the purpose, that was effectively obtained.

50. *Chaplain's removal from office.* The custom had been for the chaplain to remain in office till resigning, or for an indefinite period. This seems to be needful, if he is the right man, for it takes time for him to become acquainted with the inmates and establish himself in their confidence. Frequent changes in this office is bad policy. After serving in the place a while and finding so much interest connected with this department of labor, I decided to throw my whole energies into the work for a time and see what fruits could be gathered therefrom. I was also at no little labor and painstaking in a change of location, moving near the institution, to be in close proximity to my work. Things progressed till, a few weeks after the March election of '71, a Democratic neighbor remarked that, should his party come into power, I should have a competitor, the next summer, for my office. It was understood that the competing gentleman's plea was, that, more than twenty-five years previously, he had been appointed to the place and served nine years, but when the Democratic party lost the power, he was set aside; yet he had been living all these eventful years true to those principles, and now on the party's return to power he should be restored also to his former place. It was understood, too, that he had received the promise of the position on this contingency. The new Governor obtained his election, after which Democratic friends of the city and elsewhere assured me that my place would not be disturbed, especially as I was doing so much for the prisoners; and one of their leading men undertook to attend to the matter when the Governor and council should come to the prison questions, and present the general wish from all parties that I remain. I proceeded with my usual work for six weeks, when, just at night, one day, I received word that I had been dismissed. Directly referring this

to that gentleman, "Why," said he, "that is a mistake. This very afternoon, not two hours ago, at the council chamber, they assured me they should not act on the prison offices till their next meeting some two weeks ahead." But notwithstanding his assurances, the step was taken just on the heel of their adjournment.

On inquiring of a councilman, if, in this dismissal, they had been influenced in any measure by the aspersions in the Report, he said they had not; that they did not doubt but that I had been faithful in my duty, assuring me that the reason was wholly political; to which I had no excuse to offer, as I had been guilty of voting the Republican ticket; and if I must be dismissed on that ground, of course no more words were needed. But there did seem a lack of straightforwardness for them to move as they did in the matter without giving this gentleman the opportunity of presenting what he wished.

The gentleman appointed was a good man, but feeble, and acknowledged to a friend that he could not do what had been done for the prisoners the previous year. But the idea seemed to prevail that he could do what was desired by the warden. Hence, as is understood, the secular school is largely a thing of the past, and finally the Sabbath school is given up. Now, this is a very nice place for him in his advanced years, he being over seventy, where he has no care, and but little labor.

But what of the effects upon the inmates thus left with so much idle time on their hands? Anything but good. A young man, the previous year, was quiet and orderly, closely attentive to his studies, making good advancement; but, when left with all these unemployed moments, he turned his thoughts to planning an outbreak, was arrested in the execution, and for months condemned to the ball and chain. Whereas, had his mind been kept employed as formerly, no doubt he would have continued quiet. Does it pay thus to cut off educational and moral privileges and share such results?

---

51. *Prison fare under the new government.* I did not serve under this government for a period sufficiently long to enable me to learn from personal observation very much as to what would be gained in the fare of the prisoners, but thought some steps were being taken in the right direction. The cracked wheat dinner was abolished for meat and potatoes. The evening after, I found the prisoners rejoicing over it. One exclaimed, "*Didn't* we have a good dinner, to-day? They have put away that wheat stuff, and now give us good meat and potatoes. Oh, *isn't* it good?" A woman, leaving prison, gave us an account of the warden's scolding, that Councillor —— "was about poking his nose into everything." This, if true, gave signs of a determination to know and remedy matters. But they had to

work under difficult circumstances. They did not begin sufficiently near the bottom.

As informed, they went quite thoroughly into fitting up the clothing and bedding,—a welcome move, for no set of fellows ever needed it more. The next winter, however, I said to a man who was leaving, "You fare better over there this year than last, do you not? You are kept warmer, are you not?" To which he answered, "I don't see much difference." Certainly, I was looking for a different answer from this, and did not know what to make of it.

---

52. *The warden question.* It was supposed and reported that the warden would be removed; then we learned that the political muddle prevented, some contending for a straight, out-and-out Democrat, others, for a Labor Reformer, the party with whom they had bargained and thus gained the power. Then there was another element which seemed largely to prevail, and which some thought acted more powerfully than all others,—the fear as to how the prison accounts would stand at the end of the year. They had found out the condition of things in the prison, and learned something of how they had been run the previous year, and had every reason to suppose that they could not possibly make so large a show of gains as was then made. A highly important matter to them, for, should they run behind, their opponents would, of course, use it to their party disadvantage in future political campaigns. What could they do in the matter? Of course, the most feasible way was to keep the same warden, with the hope, by his manipulating, of a less falling off; or the fact of their having made no change here, would blunt the force of the falling-short argument materially. Hence, party interests would prompt them, on the one hand, to remove the chaplain for a partisan; and on the other to retain the warden for his aid to them politically. Thus, it seemed that party considerations ruled the whole matter, and that the rulers, instead of rising to the true dignity of their position, and inquiring about the real interests of the prison, the best man for the place, bowed obsequiously to the shrine of party. True, late in the fall, or in early winter, they moved in the matter by appointing a gentleman of Concord to the wardenship, but under such circumstances, that he could not, for a moment, think of accepting, though doubtless he would have improved matters had he done so.

---

53. *Experience at the prison subsequent to dismissal.* This experience was limited, but sufficient to open another dark chapter in the history of poor human nature. I still acted as agent to the Association. In August, a man was to leave, concerning whom they started the story that an indictment was made

against him, ready for his arrest on leaving prison; but they promised that if he would leave within a half hour after his dismissal, he could go safely. I had a place for him near a friend with whom relatives had deposited money on his account, but whose locality I supposed he did not know. Very early, on the morning of his release, I, by a message, solicited the warden to forward him to me, so that I could send him on the five o'clock train. But seeing nothing of him, I at length went to the prison office and asked the warden if he would please let the man out, as I could send him by the next train. He answered, "He has gone, Sir; went this morning at five, for New York." I now turned to the deputy as usual previously, and asked, "Will you please furnish me with a list of those going out this month?" He answered, "No, Sir;" when the warden said, "You have had enough to do with the prisoners, already. You are not to have any more concern with them." I answered, "Very well," and, turning to go out, remarked to a man about to leave, for whom I had a place in readiness, "Come to me as you leave here, and I will give you directions as to where to go." The deputy followed me, indulging in a tirade of most abusive language. As he finished the words, "You had better not be over here making a fool of yourself, but keep away lest you get kicked out," I had arrived at the top of the stairs, where I stopped, supposing he proposed to kick me down, remarking, in a subdued tone of voice, nothing frightened or excited, "Here I am. If you wish to kick me down stairs, you can. I came in civilly on business, supposing, as a citizen, I had a right to that." The deputy ejaculated, "A d——d poor citizen," the warden also having followed, and joining freely in the vituperation. Seeing no active signs of putting the threat in practice, I started on and came safely away, but was subsequently informed by one then standing at the foot of the stairs, that he kicked towards me, when I had taken a few steps. But he did not hit or injure the object of his rage. In this experience I was more fortunate than a guard, who, as he asserts, when leaving service there, was followed to the front door and kicked down the steps by the warden, upon the ground, the foot hitting his back and causing such lameness that he had not then, after four months, recovered. He was purposing to prosecute the warden for damages.

Thus, while they have smiles and words of suavity for some, they can deal freely in such abuse to those who doubt their highest perfection. Now, if they would treat me and others thus, what would they do to the prisoners? One will say, "They were irritated towards you, for you had told the Governor and Council about the prison management." That was no doubt the fact. And they will become irritated with the prisoners also, who are helplessly in their power, where they can treat them as they please.

As to the two prisoners, whether the one pretended that he would go to N. Y., and took passage accordingly, or was forced to that, I never knew.

But he would have taken passage to any place the warden proposed, in order to escape from his hands, as, through his influence, he doubtless feared the arrest. For the ticket, the warden expended the man's five dollars allowed by the State, and advanced him five more, probably supposing that it would be paid him by the Association. The man, as I learn, rode until he felt safe from being seized, when he left the cars, traveling on foot for lack of means to go by public conveyance, and, at length, arrived at this friend's, in as bad a plight, probably, as any before spoken of. He said he had been sick, confined to his cell for weeks, was neglected, and sometimes was not furnished with water to wash for days together.

The warden, himself, accompanied the second man to a place in the city, and put him to work as he had previously arranged. Soon hearing of his locality, I called, found his new pants with a bad rent, after only part of a day's wear, and furnished him with suitable clothing, pointing out the place also of my arrangement to which he could go, or remain where he was.

Another leaving prison, and calling on me, remarked, "I asked the warden where you lived, to which he answered, "I don't know;" an additional specimen of the truthfulness there.

But one queries, "Why was the warden determined that you should not see the men coming out?" He could have had but one reason, the fear that they would tell me the stories of their sufferings. The one ticketed for N. Y., I learn, gives some spicy accounts.

54. *Prison report for '72.* This claims a better financial show than that of the previous year. Thus says the warden, p. 4, "I am permitted to record another year of financial success." Then the committee, p. 10, "The financial affairs are in a highly prosperous condition. You will find, by looking at the treasurer's report, that there has been a net gain, to the State, of $5,501,03, after paying all outstanding bills, which is a greater gain than the previous year, considering the less number of convicts and the larger outlay for clothing, &c. When we consider the large appropriations that have been required from year to year to run the prison, it must be encouraging to the tax-payers of the State to know that the prison has added the two past years, $10760,20 to the revenue of the State, with no outstanding bills, and no complicated matters to embarrass the institution."

This, surely, is a glowing picture; one so greatly enjoyed by its authors, that it would seem almost too bad to spoil it by letting in a gleam from the light of truth. We see from the Report that our present managers here follow closely in the footsteps of their immediate predecessors as to their statement of financial facts, though intent on outdoing them in appearances at least. Like them, they reckon only a part of the expense in running the prison, leaving out the warden's salary, and other large items, and thus pretending the gains to be what they are not. They could equally as well have omitted the sums paid the physician, deputy, guards and overseers, thereby making the figures indicate a gain of over twenty thousand for the two years, instead of over ten thousand. The principle of statement would have been the same and equally truthful. It certainly appears as though they were straining every nerve to secure the greatest personal and party popularity on the dollar and cent question. Nor would we, by any means, censure them for that, provided they proceed with a due regard to truthfulness, the rights of the prisoner and the best interest of the State. But the people can justly require them to give these a proper place in their plannings and efforts. The pecuniary question is of high import and not to be lost sight of for a moment, but should not be allowed to swallow up every other interest with a miser's greed and with even a measure of disregard for what is really true.

In estimating the entire amount of expense to the community, this year, in running the prison, of right we should reckon a somewhat large item not above alluded to, the sum expended in caring for those made invalids the past year by the prison management, and thus sent out to the public charge. Of these there are probably six at least,—those two sent to the Insane Asylum, and four others. Thus, deducting all the real expenditures, but a small list of gains are left.

To be able the better to judge comparatively and see the drift of things in our prison management, let us select the more important items from the Reports of the years '70, '71 and '72, forming them into a table, taking the average number of the prisoners for each year, obtained by adding the numbers at its beginning and end, and dividing by two. Under the food and clothing items, let us insert what they pay in Massachusetts State Prison per day for food, and per year for clothing, to a prisoner or per capita:

		1870.		1871.		1872.	
Average number,		123	1-2	104	1-2	85	1-2
Expense for Overseers and Guards,		$5,960 03		$6,314 91		$6,613 32	
"	Physician,	100 00		250 38	1-2	282 00	1-2
"	Provisions,	8,581 32		5,416 41		3,283 00	
"	" per capita,	69 48		51 83		38 39	
"	" per day,	19		14	1-	10	1-

"	per capita,			5	2
"	" per day in Mass. Prison,	18	18	6-10	18 7-10
"	Fuel and Lights,	1,195 43	954 41		682 13
"	Clothing,	1,963 94	1,447 86		1,472 24
"	" per capita,	15 90	13 85		17 21
"	" in Mass. Prison,	21 67	19 40		18 72
"	Library,	262 95	94 84		0
"	Ordinary Repairs,	1,937 64	1,057 08		1,029 50
Earnings of Convicts,		25,338 22	22,619 70		19,134 45
"	" per capita,	209 22	216 41		223 79

This table tells its own story and is in perfect unison with all that has been uttered on former pages. The guards and overseers, the same in number, and with no additional labors, receive increased pay from year to year. Nor has there been any going up in the scale of wages outside to cause a demand for this. Nor were they more experienced and intelligent, thereby claiming higher compensation. Many were mere boys, some not overstocked with intelligence. They had one boy of seventeen for overseer in the shop.

The physician's pay has also received a yearly rise in the scale, though with a large diminishing in numbers of prisoners and, as the Report says, a remarkably healthy state among them. How can we reconcile this? True, the first year he attended only when called, and subsequently every morning. But why the difference between the second and third years with the fewer men and alleged healthy state? This is what needs explaining.

But we find the food expense going the other way,—19, 14 1-5 and 10 1-2 per day to a man. What a cutting off! Will it go on thus till the story of Hierocles about the man's horse shall be verified in our prison? So, also, of the lighting and fuel with no change of space to be warmed,—$1,195 43, $954 41 and $682 13. No wonder there was such suffering from cold that second winter, before pointed out. Then what of the third? No change in the prices of the market can account for this variance. It must have been sheer withholding the necessaries of life. We see that the Charlestown food allowance per day, for those years respectively, was,—18, 18 6-10 and 18 7-10, increasing a trifle. Nor does any great extravagance appear in that first year with us, nineteen cents, one cent lower than authors say should be, though one higher than Massachusetts.

The allowance to the library is also suggestive,—$262 95, $94 84 and 0. True, during the first year the library was repaired, enlarged and newly catalogued, but the second year the appropriation was about what is annually demanded for keeping the books properly replenished and in suitable order. It is as small a sum as should be thought of. That cypher, therefore, for the third year, shows an unwarrantable neglect. These figures are especially suggestive, too, on the educational and moral points, perhaps a good index of them. And what a show! Down, down! What a picture for New Hampshire! Grant that the chaplain preaches to the men Sabbath mornings, meets them in the prayer-meetings, &c., to what does it amount in the midst of such surroundings? True, it gratifies them to assemble, hear the human voice, and sing. That is about all the good that can be looked for under the circumstances.

The labor figures, too, are expressive,—$209 22, $216 44 and $223 79, what each earned per year; poorer fare and more work. We admit that this rise may, in part, be credited to the fact that, from the former warden's suggestion, our rulers had arranged for the doctor to visit the prison daily and examine the cases desiring excuse from work, by real or pretended sickness, with the anticipation of saving more or less labor, which that warden supposed he had lost from being left himself to do this excusing, and without medical advice, which measure commenced when the new warden came in. But, besides this, enough remains unaccounted for in that way, no doubt, to render it highly probable that too many of those complaining of having been driven to work when sick, had just cause for such complaints.

Those figures on repairs are important,—$1,937 64, $1,057 08 and $1,029 50. That first year made the last of those spent in that general fitting up, enlarging and repairing as preparatory to running the institution at more income, less expense, and, consequently, larger gains than ever before, thus laying the foundation for its present prosperity. Those sums for the second and third years would have been mere trifles but for keeping the shop appliances in repair, and that of the first very much less. Now that the contractor keeps these appliances in order himself, this repair bill for a long while to come should be very small. Hence, when we hear the laudations of the present apparent financial prosperity of the prison over that of a few years ago, we are not to infer that those former rulers were any the less shrewd, far-seeing, or energetic in financial matters than those of later date, but that the latter are only reaping from what the former sowed.

The table shows us how the increased gains are secured; mostly by withholding the necessaries of life from the men, and yet driving them to more work.

But we turn from examining this table more directly again to the Prison Report of '72. It says,—"As complaint has been made that the prisoners were not properly fed and clothed, or that the food was deficient in quantity and quality, we say to you that we think no prisoners in this country are so well fed and clothed as the convicts of the New Hampshire State Prison." What shall we think concerning the judgment of those writers? It seems that they have become conversant with the prison fare in all the States of our country, and, after careful examination, have deliberately formed the opinion that the fare in the N. H. State Prison, at ten and one-half cents per day, is really better than that elsewhere at eighteen cents.

Then again, ibid: "No article of food has been furnished by us that was not good, sweet and wholesome; and as good in quality as will average upon the tables of the tax-payers of the State. The remarkably healthy look of the convicts is plain proof that they are well cared for, have a plenty to eat, and that which is good." It seems that the authors of this part of the Report have not only traveled far and wide over our country and surveyed each prison, but have also called on every tax-payer of our State, scrutinized their tables carefully, and found that their average living costs not over ten and one-half cents per day to each individual. When found they time for all this? Or are we to understand that they are purposely using the whitewash their predecessors left?

The chaplain is again, in this Report, brought forward thus, pp. 10 and 11,—"At the commencement of our labors as Prison Committee there was a want of harmony between the former chaplain and the officers of the prison, which seemed to us against the interests of the prison, and ought, in some way, to be removed. We could see no way to obviate this difficulty other than the removal of the warden or the chaplain. After due consideration, with the best information we could get, we thought best to recommend the removal of the chaplain and the appointment of Mr. Smith to that office. By this change harmony was at once restored. Mr. Smith has rendered faithful and effective labor, to the entire satisfaction of the committee and officers of the prison. Mr. Smith's prison experience, together with the deep interest he has for the welfare of the prisoners, seems to indicate him to be the right man in the right place."

"Rather hard on the former chaplain," said one of our editors. But what shall we believe? One of the subscribers to this article told him that he was removed on purely political grounds, as previously narrated. Then there was that corroborative assertion by the democratic neighbor that Mr. Smith had received the conditional promise. Now this declaration is published to the world. Where is the truth? Were they unwilling to put it out squarely that they had made a political foot-ball of the prison? Or would they rather sacrifice the character and reputation of an innocent man, who had labored as best he could for the good of the institution? They pretend to have acted in view of a difficulty between the chaplain and warden, and "with the best information we could get, we thought best to recommend the removal of the chaplain." Where did they obtain that information? There was, of course, but one source, and, from a year's experience, the writer understands something of its character, that it would not be impossible for men regarding themselves rather shrewd to leave, wholly misconceiving the real truth. But what shall we say of this course of condemning a man unheard, and on ex parte assertions? Is that the part of honorable dealing? But the whole subject is left with the reader to pass judgment upon in view of the facts already set before him.

---

55. *International Penitentiary Congress, London, July 3-13, 1872.* This resulted from the move already spoken of at the gathering in Ohio in '70. Dr. Wines, there selected to the important work of bringing about the proposed assemblage, received due governmental qualifications by a commission from our President according to a special act of Congress, the Secretary of State also opening the way by communicating with the various governments represented at Washington, respecting the great subject. On this mission, the Dr. visited Europe in '71, received a cordial welcome from the various governments, and found them generally in readiness to enter heartily into the move. After due consultation, London was settled upon as the place of meeting, a committee, to provide for which and facilitate its general objects, was chosen in London with the Right Hon. Sir Walter Crafton as Chairman and Edwin Pears, Barrister at Law, Secretary. This committee is represented as composed of all political parties, with Lord Carnarvon really at the head, similar committees being formed in most of the other countries moving in the enterprise. To prepare work for the congress and secure its objects, a circular was addressed to the various States containing thirty prominent questions on imprisoning and its connected points, for answer. On assembling, this body found itself composed of delegates duly commissioned from twenty-two different governments, Russia and Turkey included, all the States of Europe represented but Portugal, delegates present from India, Victoria and other British colonies, South America, and eighteen of our United States, then representatives from various penitentiaries, benevolent societies for giving aid to released prisoners, magistracies, &c., &c., 298 in number, a gathering

the like of which, in some respects, had never been held. Here were judges, professors of criminal law, prison managers, philanthropists, and various gentlemen skilled in the working of criminal jurisprudence.

Here the commissioned dignitaries from kings and emperors found themselves met with delegates from voluntary associations and democratic institutions. How could they, in justice to their dignity, submit to this? But the matter was amicably adjusted, and all came upon a democratic level and acted in the greatest harmony,—an important gain to manhood. The meeting was held at a Hall of the Middle Temple; at the opening, Earl Carnarvon presiding and making the inaugural address, giving welcome to the foreign delegates and making numerous important suggestions. At the next session Dr. Wines presided, and gave an address full of information as to the purpose of calling this congress and the objects to be gained,—a universal harmony in prison managing, which managing should have certain broad principles underlying, permeating and vivifying it.

At a soiree given by the English committee to foreign visitors, the Prince of Wales and suit attended, thus showing the sanction of the English government to the congress. This sanction was also expressed by the attendance at one session of the Home Secretary of State, Right Hon. Austin H. Bruce, giving an official welcome to the gathering, and expressing a hope of being materially profited by the deliberations. The meeting, on the whole, was an important affair, of high interest from beginning to end. Its transactions are published in a volume of 796 pages, to be had of Rev. Dr. Wines, New York. Then one of the commissioners from New Hampshire, Mr. Allen Folger, wrote out a synopsis of the doings, which has been published in a pamphlet of 50 pages, by the authority of our State, for distribution, showing the interest our Governor and Council take in these matters.

The questions before spoken of were taken up by each country and elaborate answers given, papers were read upon them and thorough discussion had. The order was not to take any votes but to bring in facts of the various prison workings, to interchange views, criticise and thus sift out the best, in which, evidently, great enlightening of mind was obtained, and a great advancement made in the right direction. On page 537 of Transactions we have the following reform sentiments: "Man, in the state of penal servitude, is no longer a thing, but a moral being, whose liberty human justice has not the right to confiscate absolutely and irrevocably, but only within the limits required by the protection and security of social order. The logical sequence of this view is, that it is the duty of society to reform the criminal during his temporary privation of liberty, since, in this way only can the peril of his relapse be successfully combatted, and the public safety effectually maintained. The reformation of imprisoned criminals is not, therefore, in our day, a work of philanthropy, but an obligation of the State."

In one or two prisons they have been so successful in reform efforts, that, having taken some of the very worst criminals, they have led them to such order and good behavior, as to be able to dispense with locks and bars, rendering the prison more like a great family, kindness being the great controlling element.

In the abridged report of the proceedings of the International Congress, under the head of "Cumulative Imprisonment," we learn that the following question was submitted, and several important suggestions followed its presentation.

QUESTION: Ought prisoners on reconviction to be subjected to more severe disciplinary treatment than on the first sentence?

It was opened by M. Peterson, of Bavaria, who maintained that cases required treatment according to the degree of demerit shown on the prisoner's trial, and therefore, that instead of laying down one principle, the right course was to leave the judges to decide what should be done in each case.

M. Ploos Van Amstel, of Holland, and M. Stevens, of Belgium, advocated a merciful treatment as likely to have more effect than severity.

Mr. Aspinall, of Liverpool, read resolutions which the Liverpool magistrates had passed, to the effect that it was desirable that cumulative principles should be applied to the punishment of all crimes and offences, and that the magistrates should be empowered to transfer well conducting and deserving prisoners to homes for the remainder of their sentences. Voluminous statistics showed that there were numerous reconvictions up to seventy times, and that the conclusions arrived at, by the magistrates, was that it would be better for the prisoners and better for society if the cumulative principles were carried out.

Dr. Guillaume, of Switzerland, mentioned his experiences in some of the cantons of his country, which had led him to the conviction that it was better to give the reconvicted such sentences as would enable the prisoner to learn a trade, by which he could earn his living in the labor market without being obliged to fall back upon the lines of crime, than to give short and severe punishments, which, by including a lessened diet, sent the criminal back into the world, not only unimproved in morals, but deteriorated physically.

It would seem, according to his views, that the design of imprisoning is, to bring back to society those once injurious, but who are now changed to good citizens.

Mrs. Julia Ward Howe, of Massachusetts, advocated the merciful and kindly treatment as being the way to make a permanent impression upon the criminal classes.

M. Robin, of France, stated that his experience led him to set his face against all pains and penalties in prison, as against Christian principles, and advocated the teaching of trades. All in all, strict adherence to Christian principles should be at the bottom of the treatment of criminals.

Count de Foresta, of Italy, held that the question was rather one of law than prison discipline. He urged that there was a line of prison discipline beyond which it was impossible to go without turning the discipline into cruelty.

Another question touching "Prison Labor," was brought forward and considered, as follows:

QUESTION: "Should prison labor be merely penal, or should it be industrial?"

It was opened by the reading of a long and interesting paper by Mr. Frederick Hill, brother of the late celebrated Recorder of Birmingham. The substance of the paper was that labor, to be made useful and productive, follows natural laws, which are the same in prison as out of prison; that it is an advantage to the prisoner to fit him for usefulness and to make more easy his reform; that it will help pay the cost of his conviction and imprisonment; that upon release, he will be better armed against relapse into crime, as well as much better prepared to obtain an honest living than those whose labor has been merely penal; that the pains and privations necessarily attendant on the process of moral reformation are so great as to make it unnecessary, for the maintenance of the principle of deterrence, to superadd artificial pains and penalties.

Colonel Colville, Governor of Colbath Fields Prison, one of the largest London prisons, spoke very strongly against the tread-mill system of punishment which is in nearly all the prisons of England, and almost unanimously condemned by the prison officials.

The general opinion of the Congress was in conformity to views expressed by the speakers mentioned.

Under the question touching the moral value of visitation of the prisons by women, we find the following sensible views expressed:

"While the character of the visiting women depends upon chance, they are as likely to be indiscreet, and to interfere unwisely as otherwise. If they were selected as men are, or ought to be, for their fitness, their work would be done with good judgment and discretion. Then, again, criminal men separated from their families and from all gentle influences, need the ministry of good women for their reformation. The motherly influence of pure, gentle women will sometimes control and subdue the violent, when even blows would fail to do so."

The whole force of the International Congress went in favor of the idea of *reforming* the prisoners. For this the body advocated stimulating the prisoners' self-interest, thus:

"In this way, the prisoner's destiny during his incarceration should be placed, measurably, in his own hands; he must be put into circumstances where he will be able, through his own exertions, to continually better his condition. A regular self-interest must be brought into play. In the prison, as in free society, there must be the stimulus of some personal advantage accruing from the prisoner's efforts. Giving prisoners an interest in their industry and good conduct tends to give them beneficial thoughts and habits, and what no severity of punishment will enforce a moderate personal interest will readily obtain."

They also advocated using the moral force:

"In criminal treatment, moral forces should be relied on with as little admixture of physical force as may be; organized persuasion to the utmost extent possible should be made to take the place of coercive restraint, the object being to make upright and industrious *freemen*, rather than orderly and obedient *prisoners*. Brute force may make good prisoners, moral training alone will make good citizens. To the latter of those ends the living soul must be won; to the former, only the inert and obedient body. To compass the reformation of criminals, the military type in prison management must be abandoned, and a discipline by moral forces substituted in its place. The objects of military discipline and prison discipline, being directly opposed to each other, can not be pursued by the same road. The one is meant to train men to act together, the other to prepare them to act separately. The one relies upon force, which never yet created virtue; the other on motives, which are the sole agency for attaining moral ends. The special object of the one is to suppress individual character and reduce all to component parts of a compact machine; that of the other is to develop and strengthen individual character, and, by instilling right principles, to encourage and enable it to act on these independently."

They tell us again "that the self-respect of the prisoner should be cultivated to the utmost and every effort be made to give back to him his manhood."

"There is no greater mistake in the whole compass of penal discipline, than its studied imposition of degradation as a part of punishment. Such imposition destroys every better impulse and aspiration. It crushes the weak, irritates the strong and indisposes all to submission and reform. It is trampling, where it ought to raise, and is therefore as unchristian in principle as it is unwise in policy."

Farther, "The system of prison discipline must gain the will of the convict. He is to be amended, but this is impossible with his mind in a state of hostility. No system can hope to succeed which does not secure this harmony of wills, so that the prisoner shall choose for himself what his officer chooses for him. But to this end the officer must really choose the good of the prisoner, and the prisoner must remain in his choice long enough for virtue to become a habit. This consent of will is an essential condition of reformation, for a bad man can never be made good against his will. Nowhere can reformation become the rule instead of the exception, where this choice of the same things by prison keepers and prison inmates has not been attained."

They assert, too, that the officers should possess a hearty desire and intention to accomplish the object of reform in the prison. Regarding these officers they also say thus:

"In order to the reformation of imprisoned criminals, there must also be in the minds of prison officers a serious conviction that they are capable of being reformed, since no man can heartily pursue an object at war with his inward beliefs; no man can earnestly strive to accomplish what in his heart he despairs of accomplishing. Doubt is the prelude of failure; confidence a guaranty of success. Nothing so weakens moral forces as unbelief; nothing imparts to them such vigor as faith. 'Be it unto thee according to thy faith,' is the statement of a fundamental principle of success in all human enterprises, especially when our work lies within the realm of mind and morals."

Finally, they assure us that "work, education and religion (including in this latter moral instruction) are the three great forces to be employed in the reformation of criminals."

CONCLUSION.

The two systems of prison management, previously alluded to, are now before the reader so far as these pages have elucidated, the *reformatory* on the one hand, and the *punitive and money-making* on the other. And which do you prefer? Will your choice be for the honest effort to raise up the fallen, to do our duty to the erring, to throw what influences can be about these disturbers of society to lead them to become upright citizens? Or, will it fall upon the crushing, cruel, vindictive course, the process of making them more debased, sordid, revengeful? Do you prefer manhood-producing with its benign effects, or money-making attended with the blighting of the higher aspirations of the soul? This subject has been taken up in the narrative form, that the writer could the more easily, by incidents, and in the briefest way, bring out the peculiarities of the two systems in their workings and the animus impelling them. He has brought forward nothing in the line of facts and incidents except what had come under his own observation, or been so reported to him that he had no doubt of its truthfulness. Many of the incidents in Part II. he would gladly have passed in silence, regretting exceedingly the necessity of bringing them out. But a solemn sense of duty seemed to impel him to this task. He has delayed any move hoping the turn of events would excuse him from penning these truths for the public eye. But his conscience and his God will condemn him, if longer delayed. He has brought forward names with no unkind feeling, or purpose to expose or wound, but to show the way things have moved. No matter what course others may have taken towards him, he has endeavored studiously to follow the exhortation he has so often given to the prisoners in yielding all that into the hands of God, for his disposal.

This matter is now before the people. Will you not study the questions carefully and act? Will not ministers of religion and of law, merchants and artisans, all those in the various industries of life, men and women come to the help? True, the latter, however pure and exalted, is now forbidden entrance to the chapel in labors of love for the fallen men. Hence, that somewhat recent shock to the community in the stern refusal of Elizabeth Comstock's request for permission to address the inmates on their moral and religious interests. How long shall such things be in our prison? How long shall the light of science, of morality and of pure religion be virtually shut out from that abode? How long shall we work so as to make bad men worse, hard hearts harder, the depraved more iniquitous, the pestiferous more destructive to the safety and quietness of society? Till the people shall stir effectively, make their voice heard and their power felt. Why not change our system of imprisoning and put it fully on that of reform? Why not adopt the course of dismissing prisoners only on condition of good evidence of reform and on further condition of being returned in case of relapse into crime? Why not arrange for those who will not reform, as some will not, to serve in prison for life, thus freeing society of their depradations? Then why not use them humanely while keeping their time occupied in useful employment, still permitting each to enjoy the means of mental, moral and religious culture. Many, thus situated would, no doubt, live really good, pious lives, who, from their moral weakness, could not resist the temptations to crime which are met on every hand without. To such, the prison should act as a kind, beneficent guardian.

Milton Keynes UK
Ingram Content Group UK Ltd.
UKHW030625061024
449204UK00004B/309